WRESTLING WITH THE ANGEL

ALSO BY ENOCH POWELL

The Rendel Harris Papyri 1936
First Poems 1937
A Lexicon to Herodotus 1938
The History of Herodotus 1939
Casting-off, and other poems 1939
Herodotus, Book VIII 1939
Llyfr Blegywryd (with Stephen Williams) 1942
Thucydidis Historia 1942
Herodotus (translation) 1949
One Nation (jointly) 1950
Dancer's End and The Wedding Gift (poems) 1951
The Social Services: Needs and Means (jointly)
Change is Our Ally (jointly) 1954
Biography of a Nation (with Angus Maude) 1955
Great Parliamentary Occasions 1960
Saving in a Free Society 1960
A Nation not Afraid 1965
Medicine and Politics 1966
The House of Lords in the Middle Ages (with Keith Wallis) 1968
Freedom and Reality 1969
The Common Market: the Case Against 1971
Still to Decide 1972
Common Market: Re-negotiate or Come Out 1973

WRESTLING
WITH THE ANGEL

Enoch Powell

SHELDON PRESS
LONDON

First published in Great Britain in 1977 by
Sheldon Press, Marylebone Road, London NW1 4DU

Copyright © 1977 Enoch Powell

Filmset in 'Monophoto' Times 11 on 13 pt. and
printed in Great Britain by
Fletcher & Son Ltd., Norwich

ISBN 0 85969 127 6

CONTENTS

ACKNOWLEDGEMENTS

The author and the publisher wish to acknowledge their thanks to *The Daily Telegraph Magazine* (Easter 1976) for permission to reproduce the hymn on p. xi, to *The Times* for permission to reproduce *No Cradle at the Inn* (24 December 1973) and *Christianity and the Curse of Cain* (14 July 1973), to the BBC World Service for *Where do we go from here?* (17 March 1974), to BBC Television for *The God who Hides Himself* (14 March 1975), to *The Liberal Catholic* for *The Archaeology of Matthew* (June 1975, Vol. XLIV No. 2 and September–December 1975, Vol. XLIV Nos. 3 and 4), to Bryan Magee and London Weekend Television for the dialogue *Christianity and Social Activity* (23 January 1973), and to the *Sunday Express* for *I Believe*. *God Save the Queen* and *Patriotism* were given at St Lawrence Jewry, London, on 26 November 1974 and 18 January 1977 respectively. *Action for World Development* was given at the A.G.M. of the Wolverhampton South West Conservative Association on 5 December 1969. *My Country, Right or Wrong* was given at the International Night of the Shrewsbury Round Table on 7 February 1975. *The Paradox of Personal Liberty* was given at Worth Abbey on 23 January 1976. *The Notion of Immortality* was preached at St Bartholomew's, Haslemere on 1 September 1974. *Then Shall the End Come* was given at SS Michael, Paul and Mary, Southwark, London on 11 March 1973. *Bibliolatry* was given at the Festival of the Church of England Men's Society, Carlisle, at Grange-over-Sands on 14 July 1973. *The Feeding of the Five Thousand* was preached at St Peter's, Eaton Square, London on 17 February 1974. *The Woman taken in Adultery* was preached in Bessbrook Barracks, Co Armagh on 16 March 1975.

vii

FOREWORD

This is a different book from *No Easy Answers*. Though it is likewise an assemblage of articles, sermons and dialogues on particular occasions, those in this book are almost all the product of no more than three years' thinking, writing and speaking, whereas the previous collection spanned about fifteen years. Still, this is a sequel to *No Easy Answers* in that I have the sense of having gone on from where I left off there. The three years were not only years of intense personal vicissitude; they were also a period when there was hardly a single day on which one or other of the themes in the book was absent from my mind.

I am aware how deceptive the impression of movement can be. We sit in a stationary train, and the departure of the train on another line makes us think that our own journey has started. Yet, mistakenly or not, I do think that I have been travelling.

The principal change that I believe I notice is that words of the Gospel which previously I took as given starting-points for comparison or contrast with conventional morality or conventional Christianity now present themselves to me in a more and more mysterious guise, as if they themselves were rather the end-products of processes or chains of events of which I can as yet form only a dim conception. The absolutes which they address to me are no less imperious than before—the dialogue with Bryan

Magee (Chapter 7) could as well have been in the former book as in this—but the Christ who confronts me with those absolutes has become more and more like a traveller from an unknown country, whom, if I dared, I would fain question whence and how he came hither.

His light now casts behind each word the shadow of a mystery. His every action now looms huge, like the Spectre of the Brocken—except that I am sure it is no trick of light which is throwing my own figure on the screen of shifting mist. When I wrote *No Easy Answers* I could not have written 'Bibliolatry' (Chapter 14) nor 'The God Who Hides Himself' (Chapter 17). Jacob wrestled with the angel until daybreak (Gen. 32.24ff.) and forced from him a blessing but not his name: 'Wherefore is it,' replied the angel, 'that thou dost ask after my name?' But Jacob concluded: 'I have seen God face to face, and my life is preserved.' I find the allegory compelling. We cannot choose but wrestle with the nameless stranger, though he will not yield his secret to us in the form in which we seek it. As if the prize were 'to see God face to face', there is no desisting—until the day breaks.

March 1977.   J. ENOCH POWELL.

AN EASTER HYMN

As once the sacrificial blood
On doors and lintel posts
Brought Israel scatheless through the flood
And scattered Egypt's hosts,

So now, transfigured yet the same,
The victim-victor priest
His own once more has come to claim,
From Death's dark land released.

For see! The doors were locked, but he
The unhoped, unlooked-for guest
Entered among us suddenly
And took the bread and blessed;

And though the drear infinity
Of desert stretches sore
The whole way hence to Galilee,
Where he is gone before,

We doubt not but his saving hand
And presence us shall meet
When on the border of that land
Death's waters wash our feet.

1

PATRIOTISM

When the Rector asked me to return to this rostrum to speak about patriotism, I would fain have declined if it were possible to refuse anything that Basil Watson[1] asks. The subject is too daunting, whichever way one approaches it. If you tackle it philosophically, it dissolves into dry-as-dust definitions and refinements. If you tackle it theologically, I fear you end up in the New Jerusalem, which, after all, is rather a different subject. If you tackle it head-on, slap-happy wise, you are apt to travel around a circular argument of self-congratulation, making the kind of hearty speech demanded at old school or regimental occasions.

The only way out I have found is to tell some fragments of my own story as best I can. If at the end you think I have said anything about patriotism, that will be your responsibility, not mine. The person who claims to be a patriot is as much to beware of as the person who assures you he is honest.

I am probably mistaken in imagining that I remember the battles of the Coronel and Falkland Islands at the time they happened, though the impressions of Jack Cornwell V.C. in his shattered gun turret and of the invincibility (as it proved) of H.M.S. *Invincible* must have made their mark not long after these events. But the first recollections that I

---

[1] Rector of St Lawrence Jewry, London.

have of nation as the object of loyalty and affection date from after the First World War, which ended when I was six, and are connected with the English monarchy. Through my childhood and adolescence the land and the buildings of England and Wales were perceived by me always somehow in a fourth dimension, the dimension of time, as if they were the stage and scenery of the long epic of the English kings. The predominant role of the monarchy and its bearers was as unifiers: they seemed to be the nation-creators, and later the empire-creators, both actively, by force and policy, and passively, as the unifying focus of sentiment and the source of lawful authority.

Right up to and through the Second World War the assumption, present without being reasoned, that all other aims and values were subordinate to preserving the empire-nation from the destruction threatened by its enemies, was personalized and rationalized in terms of allegiance. That this was so I not only recollect but can verify from poetry written when on service in North Africa and India. Westminster in these was the place not of Parliament but of monarchy, the place where the hallowed dust of the Plantagenets still exercised symbolic power.

I suppose that the five years after I touched down on English soil again in February 1946 were a period of more drastic change and revision of ideas than I ever experienced before or since. There was first the ending of the Indian Empire. Not only physically but psychologically it was from India that I had made the transition from war into politics as a lifetime's profession; and now straightaway the ground crumbled under my feet. If neither in India nor in Britain there was the will to sustain the common allegiance, there was no such thing as a nation-empire, and not merely no Indian Empire but no Empire at all, nothing of lasting substance beyond the coasts of the

British Isles themselves. That conclusion, and the conviction that it was the outcome not of mischance or failure but of necessity, was gradually borne in upon me when, little more than a year afterwards, I was endeavouring—unsuccessfully—to induce my then employers, the Conservative Party, to have nothing to do with the British Nationality Act of 1948.

That Act destroyed the status of British subject based on allegiance and substituted the sum total of the local citizenships with which the former parts of the Empire—Canada in the van—had provided themselves or would provide themselves in future. The result was a Commonwealth consisting of a few ex-British nations with the same titular sovereign as the United Kingdom, and a much larger number of non-British republics. The common status was reduced to a nullity. The whole contraption was a humbug, a pretence and a self-deception; and I came to hate it. Neither I nor anyone else could then foresee the nemesis of massive New Commonwealth immigration into England which was to be the direct consequence of this fiction that common status could still exist when common allegiance and common authority had ceased.

So by the early '50s, despite the long story of colonial disentanglement which still lay ahead, it was for me as if the nation and the monarchy had come back home again. Without ever losing, to this hour, the old sense of the symbolic, numinous kingship, I had now understood that the sovereign was not the Crown in abstract but the Crown in Parliament—and not in Parliament in general, nor in a parliament here, a parliament there and a parliament somewhere else, but in the Parliament of the United Kingdom, or, to name it less exactly but more truthfully, the English Parliament. Herein lay the necessity of the limitation of the nation and the allegiance to those who

3

physically, politically and spiritually could be represented in Parliament. It was the key which interpreted our past imperial history and accurately forecast how its terminal stages would run.

It would be true to say that all the major causes in politics to which I have devoted myself in the last twenty years and more have grown for me out of two convictions: that the nation is the one social unit which, on the secular plane at least, provides a satisfying frame of reference for men's individual hopes and ambitions; and that the only nation I can recognize as my own is that defined by allegiance to the Crown in Parliament or, alternatively stated, that which voluntarily, cheerfully and instinctively recognizes the authority of Parliament as exclusive and supreme. Subjects apparently the most diverse are for me aspects or applications of a central dedication to these beliefs. I will touch in a moment upon three or four such subjects to illustrate what I mean. I will look at Commonwealth immigration and at Ulster unionism, at policies of economic dependence and at membership of the European Economic Community, opposition to which has dictated the severance of all political ties that might interfere with it. Before I do so, however, let me confess and record a paradox which I think is relevant.

During the twenty-seven years that the House of Commons has been, almost literally, my home, I have grown simultaneously more convinced of its indispensable centrality to the life of the nation and more dubious and even critical of its actual condition and spirit and of the motivation and self-respect of its membership. I could almost dare to say with the Psalmist (69.9), 'the zeal of thine house hath eaten me up, and the reproaches of them that reproached thee are fallen upon me'. Of course, as with any decent paradox, there is no real contradiction.

PATRIOTISM

The more vital the institution, the greater the temptation to idealize, and the harder it becomes to match the ideal with the reality.

Though legend relates otherwise, I would not have chosen, if I could have avoided it, to become the eponymous exponent of the conviction that by no contrivance can the prospective size and distribution of our population of 'New Commonwealth ethnic origin'—the expression is not mine but that of the Office of Population Censuses and Surveys—prove otherwise than destructive of this nation. The basis of my conviction is neither genetic nor eugenic; it is not racial, because I can never discover what 'race' means and I have never arranged my fellow men on a scale of merit according to their origins. The basis is political. It is the belief that self-identification of each part with the whole is the one essential pre-condition of being a parliamentary nation, and that the massive shift in the composition of the population of the inner metropolis and of major towns and cities of England will produce, not fortuitously or avoidably, but by the sheer inevitabilities of human nature in society, ever increasing and more dangerous alienation. There is no individual, however remote and strange his background and origins, who could not choose and achieve the self-identification which is the touchstone of belonging to a nation. But from the individual to the millions there runs no line of analogy or deduction. If I could believe otherwise, I would; but I cannot.

Self-identification as the touchstone of nationhood was the conviction which over seven years ago, before it was imaginable to me or anyone else that I could cease of my own volition to sit in Parliament for a Staffordshire seat, obliged me—almost alone among English Members—to enrol in the cause of Ulster Unionism, though I had no personal connections with that province. From the beginning of the disturbances it was clear to me that here was a population of whom the majority desired beyond any other political end to remain part of this nation but whom their enemies and those who should have been their friends were combining to crucify for the offence of being and wishing to be British. Their enemies, who used the most modern techniques to terrorize and overwhelm them, were less dangerous than the Government, Parliament and political parties of their own countrymen, who spent seven years in the fatal search for an impossibility—a compromise between belonging to one nation and belonging to another nation so as equally to satisfy those whose hearts are set upon the one and upon the other. It is Britain's attempt to deny in Northern Ireland the reality of nationhood that is ultimately the cause of so much bloodshed, suffering and distraction. People sometimes ask me: 'How does it feel to be an M.P. in Ulster, a stranger in a strange land, after a quarter of a century spent representing your own folk in England?' I reply: 'No different at all. I sit in the same Parliament, I represent a part of the same nation, I serve the same cause.'

Perhaps it was more than accident that the Britain which would fain have denied to one of its provinces the right to be part and parcel of the nation was a Britain engaged, during those very same years, in denying that it had any right or desire to remain a nation at all itself. A victorious continental enemy, determined to absorb this United Kingdom into its dominions, could not have dictated at Westminster a more comprehensively humiliating surrender than the Act which Parliament passed in 1972 in order that this country should become part of the European Economic Community. It enacted that the laws of an external authority should prevail over our domestic laws, it gave an external authority the power to legislate and tax without the consent of Parliament, it placed in the hands of that external authority the whole control of Britain's trade. Moreover, those who counselled it did so on the express ground that Britain was obsolete as a nation state. Wilhelm II could not have demanded so much; I doubt if Hitler would have demanded more. I can still only half believe that I was myself an unwilling witness to my country's abnegation of its own national independence.

The fact that I do not impugn the honour or sincerity of those who throughout the ages have thought that national independence can be too dearly bought, does not release me from obeying the contrary conviction. I am not to know whether it is destined that my fellow countrymen will be contented with the status of a European province and will accept that henceforward this nation is unworthy or incapable of being an independent sovereign state like Iceland or Zambia. I did not know when I came home from Australia in September 1939 whether these islands could defend themselves against the German armies and air-fleets. To be impelled to fight for one's country it is not necessary to be certain that one's country is going to win. I only say that I will never accept as *fait accompli* the renunciation of our national independence and the destruction of our parliamentary sovereignty which took place in 1972.

I have shot past the miserable present. For over twenty years of my public life a large part of my thought and study has gone to advocacy of those self-regulating mechanisms which it has become customary to describe as 'the market'. In fact it was in this context that the expressions 'Powellite' and 'Powellism' were current for years before something called 'race' reared its head in the political vocabulary. On this theme, from the days when I roused City audiences to ribald laughter by proving to them that it was possible—nay, desirable—for the exchange rate of the pound to 'float', down to these last months in Parliament when I protested against Britain borrowing a single dollar from the I.M.F. or the international bankers, my true motivation has been as thoroughly nationalist as in my exposition of Ulster Unionism or my antagonism to E.E.C. membership. We, this nation, have a right, because we are such, to formulate and follow the standards by which we will judge the worth of what we do and of what others offer to us and expect from us. In matters material—and their boundary with matters not material is frequently invisible—we cannot do that, if political compulsion, whether internal, of our own government, or external, of a cabal and conspiracy of other governments, is allowed to fix the terms in which we assess that lesser part of value which is measurable. The breath which condemns submission to laws this nation has not made condemns submission to scales of value which this nation has not willed. To both sorts of submission I ascribe that haunting fear, which I am sure I am not alone in feeling, that we, the British will soon have nothing left to die for.

That was not a slip of the tongue. What a man lives for is what a man dies for, because every bit of living is a bit of dying. At the beginning I refused to define patriotism; but now at the end I venture it. Patriotism is to have a nation to die for, and to be glad to die for it—all the days of one's life.

2

NO CRADLE AT THE INN

The Christmas deluge of mangers and stables and animals around the crib in every conceivable pose and situation is in flood. It is accompanied by all those sermons, which, not satisfied with the truth that the Saviour 'came to visit us in great humility' [1], must fain inform us that he was born in a stable among the cattle because the rich and the heartless had left 'no room at the inn' for Joseph and Mary. It will go hard if there is not many a reference to Rachman and property speculators and housing shortage.

All which comes of not reading the Bible, which says nothing at all about Jesus being born in a stable. 'What?' you exclaim. 'Surely the Gospel tells how Joseph and Mary coming to Bethlehem found no room at the inn and so sought shelter in a stable, where the child was born?' Nothing of the sort, though generation after generation has thought that that was what the Gospel said. The narrative comes only in Luke (Chap. 2), who preferred it to that of the wise men and star, which by then had become so overlaid in Matthew with alterations and additions as to be confused and puzzling.

'And Joseph too returned from Galilee from the city of Nazareth to Judaea to the city of David which is called Bethlehem, because he was of the house and line of David, to register along with Mary his betrothed, who was

[1] The Advent collect.

9

pregnant.' Nothing about rooms and stables so far. 'And it came to pass during the time they were there'—they spent some days at least in Bethlehem—'her time to be delivered was fulfilled, and she bore her firstborn son, and she wrapped him up and laid him'—where? not, as would be normal, in a cradle, but—'in a feeding-trough'.

Now, a feeding-trough closely resembles in shape a wooden cradle, its only drawback for serving as such being that it is apt to be too big. This, however, can be remedied by wrapping the child up in a thick bundle, which is the point of mentioning what we translate as the 'swaddling clothes'. If this had been just the standard procedure, there would have been no more point in mentioning it than in saying that the child was washed and fed, nor, unless it was exceptional, would the angel have treated it, along with the feeding-trough, as part of the sign which he gave to the shepherds.

But why put the baby in a feeding-trough? The answer is obvious. As the parents were away from home, and therefore had no cradle, which was part of the permanent furnishing of every family home, it was the handiest substitute. That must be the sense of the words, or whatever lies behind the words, 'because they had no place at the inn'. The clause is there to explain why Jesus was put in a feeding-trough (which the narrative has just stated), and not why he was born in a stable (which the narrative nowhere suggests). What the words cannot mean is that the 'inn' was full and therefore the parents had been housed in a stable. The difficulty about where to put the baby would have been the same whether they were accommodated inside the 'inn' or outside. That difficulty, quite simply, was not having a cradle. In fact, the word 'inn' is a translation with misleading implications; for the word which it renders means no more than 'somewhere to stay'—

10

'caravanserai' would be less inaccurate—and curiously, the words 'at the inn' do not appear at all in the Syriac.

Thus was produced the sign by which the angel accredited his announcement to the shepherds: 'In case you don't believe me, I can tell you that you'll find the baby bundled up in a feeding-trough.' Only a supernatural messenger could have known that curious detail. It is exactly the sort of sign—an exceptional circumstance, due to simple chance but identifying the hero—which is a staple feature of folklore.[2]

The 'feeding-trough' was soon connected with the verse of Isaiah (1.3): 'The ox knoweth his master and the ass his master's crib, but Israel doth not know, my people doth not consider.' Accordingly one ox and one ass, looking at the child in the crib, appear in the representations of the nativity as early as the fourth century, and follow right through the Middle Ages, till a more naturalistic fancy began to demand a real stable scene.

The stable and the attendant cattle and the hard-hearted innkeeper—anyhow, why *was* he hard-hearted, if the 'inn' was in fact full up?—have had a long history. We should all be sorry to have gone without them. But what those who use them to point a moral cannot claim for them is the authority of the Gospel.

[2] Moreover the 'ark' (Exod. 2.3) in which Moses, the giver of the First Law, was laid as a baby was the 'type' of the receptacle of the infant giver of the Second Law. This may be seen, for instance, among other 'types' in the window of the chapel at Hatfield House.

3

CHRISTIANITY AND THE CURSE OF CAIN

'God's unequivocal yes to man's conscience-ridden question "Am I my brother's keeper?" is the basis of all Jewish and all Christian morality.'

That was the first sentence of the Revd Paul Oestreicher's article in *The Times* of 7 July 1973 under the title 'Blood on whose hands in Mozambique?'

It would be unfortunate if that were 'the basis of all Jewish and all Christian morality', because it happens simply not to be true. Anyone who takes the trouble, so unfashionable nowadays among the clergy, to read the Bible will discover that the implied answer to the question, so far from being 'an unequivocal yes', is actually 'no'.

Cain, we are told in Genesis (4.9), 'rose up against his brother Abel and slew him'. Then God said to Cain: 'Where is Abel thy brother?' Cain's surly and evasive retort, such as a suspect, after cautioning, might make to the police, was: 'I know not: am I my brother's keeper?' To this the implied response is: 'Not at all; but you know very well where he is, because you have murdered him'; and in fact God did reply: 'the voice of thy brother's blood crieth unto me from the ground'.

Thus a vivid piece of dramatic dialogue has been twisted—and countless times before Mr Oestreicher—to convey something which it never meant nor could mean, and we have been invited uncritically to accept a non-assertion as 'the basis of all Jewish and all Christian morality'.

The only moral instruction conveyed by the passage is that one ought not to murder one's own brother: fratricide is a crime. God would never talk such nonsense as to tell us that we are each 'our brother's keeper', whether in the literal sense of 'brother' or in its extension (for which the passage gives no warrant) to cover some, or all of the rest, of mankind.

For one thing, if I am my brother's keeper, it follows that he is my keeper too; and there will be a fine old quarrel between us to settle which of us is to 'keep' the other. It is only the arrogant neo-colonialism of those like Mr Oestreicher which dares to assume that the rich are to be the 'keepers' of the poor, the civilized of the savage, the overdeveloped of the underdeveloped.

But the absurdity does not end there. If I am to be 'my brother's keeper', I must literally have my brother in charge. No one can be responsible for what he does not control. Therefore, if I am to be held responsible for my brother's welfare, safety and standard of living, I must be given control over him, as a parent or guardian has control over a minor. The misconceived ordinance is thus a prescription for paternalist tyranny. It is not the same as 'loving' my brother (or 'the brethren'), but the very opposite; for to love one's brother must be to wish to treat him as one would wish to be treated oneself, that is, as a free responsible agent.

Mr Oestreicher is as entitled as anyone else to form his conclusions about what happens in Mozambique or Siberia, to voice his censure on such crimes as may be committed in one part of the globe or the other, and to recommend accordingly to Her Majesty's Government. He is not entitled to pray in aid Genesis 4.9.

4

ACTION FOR WORLD DEVELOPMENT

In churches and elsewhere throughout the country people are being urged to 'sign-in'—the very word should be a warning—to an address to Members of Parliament issued by a body called 'Churches' Action for World Development'. The declaration, which consists of four propositions, was sent to me as the Member of Parliament on behalf of the Wolverhampton Council of Christian Churches. After considering it, I replied that I regarded every one of the assertions in the declaration as meaningless and absurd, and that in my opinion the promulgation of such declarations does no good and may do some harm.

I feel this is a proper opportunity for me to expand upon what I said. Let me take the propositions one by one. First 'that mass hunger, disease and illiteracy are intolerable anywhere in the world'. Certainly hunger and disease, whether 'mass' or not, are evils which no normal person gladly contemplates others suffering; and illiteracy, though not in itself an evil, is in many circumstances a handicap. But what is meant by declaring these things to be 'intolerable'? Presumably the person signing the statement means that he does not 'tolerate' them. That, however, is either meaningless or absurd: the statement, 'I, John Smith of Wolverhampton, do not tolerate mass hunger, disease and

14

illiteracy in China or Patagonia' is nonsense—even if it makes John Smith feel good.

The second proposition is 'that the skills and resources to change these unjust conditions now exist'. I am not going to spend more than a moment on the silly but dangerous adjective 'unjust'. To say, for instance, that for the population of a territory to increase faster than its means of subsistence is 'unjust', is an absurdity. But it is worse than absurd. It does harm, because it uses as vacuous and meaningless a word which, in its proper context, has a very precise and important meaning; and those who apply the term to the automatic consequences of impersonal causes are contributing, so far as in them lies, to weaken our perception of wrong deliberately done by some members of a society to others in contravention or disregard of law and custom. However, apart from the adjective 'unjust', the statement itself is futile. In the present it is untrue: the food to raise the level of nourishment of all mankind to that of Western Europe does not, in fact, exist— is not, in fact, being produced. The meaning must be that the present behaviour of mankind could be so altered as to eliminate mass hunger, disease and illiteracy. As a theoretical statement, assuming human behaviour to be alterable at will, I imagine this is true. But the statement is not worth making without considering whether, and if so how, the present patterns of human behaviour could in fact be altered by those making the declaration and those to whom it is addressed.

So we come to the third proposition: 'to obtain justice among men the international financial and trading system can and must be changed'. Here we come to the heart of the mischief. What on earth do the persons, clerical or lay, who invite people to affirm this proposition think they are talking about? Are they talking about the Bretton Woods system of fixed exchange rates? That surely must be included. And how is it to be changed? By changing to floating exchange rates, by revaluing gold, by creating more Special Drawing Rights? The Wolverhampton Council of Christian Churches does not explain either what it means (if it has thought about the matter at all) or what it intends the signatory to mean. Then the reference to the 'trading system'. Now, this country has a trading system which includes, among other things, Commonwealth preference, but the question is now in agitation whether we should enter a different trading system, that of the European Common Market with internal free trade but external tariffs. Is this the change the Wolverhampton Council of Christian Churches means, and if so, why, and if not, what other change?

These are indeed important matters, matters on which this Member of Parliament has thought it right to form and to express opinions. An individual Methodist, Anglican or Presbyterian, whether cleric or layman, may indeed hold opinions on these matters; but he will not hold one or the other because he is a Methodist, Anglican or Presbyterian or indeed because he is a Christian. I defy anybody to decide on Christian principles for or against joining the Common Market, for or against Special Drawing Rights, for or against a floating mark compared with a revalued mark. Yet these are the very essence of what 'the international financial and trading system' is about. It is an insult to the public for the Wolverhampton Council of Christian Churches to invite them to sign a declaration that the system 'can and must be changed'; first because it neither is nor can be any business of the Wolverhampton Council of Christian Churches, and secondly, because the statement, like those before, is perfectly empty of content.

16

The answer certainly is not to be found in the fourth proposition: 'that as a first step the poorer countries must obtain more aid, and that the terms of international trade must no longer discriminate in favour of the rich'. Aid, in any case, is perfectly consistent with any number of different international financial and trading systems. There are today, as there have been during the last twenty years, two opposing views on the effect of 'aid', which I am using in its strict sense of resources raised compulsorily by one government and transferred, either cheaply or gratis, to another government, whether or not through an intermediate agency. One view, and it is held increasingly widely, is that aid is harmful to the recipient countries because, among other reasons, it results in misdirection of their economic effort and in repression of domestic saving and investment. I am not here concerned with whether this view—I happen to hold it myself—is right or wrong. The point is that it is held in good faith by large numbers of economists and others in many countries, who are just as humane in outlook as those who disagree with them. The decision between the two views is not capable of being taken on moral grounds; it depends on economic evidence, on economic theory and on economic beliefs. It is therefore either ignorant or dishonest of the Council of Churches to invite all and sundry to subscribe to one view rather than the other, as though it were implicit either in the three preceding propositions or in any of the principles of religion or morality.

In fact religion and morality are by definition excluded from aid, because aid involves compulsion, and involuntary acts have no religious or moral connotation. I can of my charity voluntarily empty my pocket into the collecting bin of Oxfam; that is, or may be, a moral act, and I may do it in the belief that I am complying with a tenet of my religion. It is not a charitable act if I pay my income tax as an alternative to going to prison, even in the knowledge that a fraction of the out-turn is going to be transferred to an international agency. Those who advocate aid or more aid do so not in order to be charitable themselves but in order to bring compulsion to bear upon others to perform what, in the case of those others, cannot be a moral act. As for Christianity, I confess it seems to me little short of blasphemy to seek arguments from it in favour of a compulsory levy of one per cent rather than 0·7 per cent. Whatever Christianity is about, it is not about decimal fractions of a percentage point.

Finally, there is the other half of the fourth proposition, about the 'terms of international trade'. If those who drafted these statements knew the first thing about the economic language they were writing, they would know that 'terms of trade' cannot 'discriminate': they are the expression of the relative value which people place on different goods and services and they change when that valuation changes. At the point of trade or exchange, there is neither rich nor poor: each party is exchanging what he values less for what he values more. Trade, like Shakespeare's mercy, 'blesseth him that gives and him that takes'. Meaning can be given to the proposition only if it is intended that governments should compulsorily alter the terms of trade by forcing their subjects to pay more for the products of certain other countries than the price at which supply and demand would otherwise have balanced. A more crude as well as foolish proposal could hardly be framed, because the inevitable result must be to reduce demand for the products of those countries—and consequently their prospects of obtaining by exchange what they prefer—and encouraging the products of other countries including our own. Nothing would suit Lancashire better than for the terms of trade to move in favour of Hong Kong or Pakistan.

You may think that I have relished the opportunity to dissect a piece of woolly thinking and self-righteous nonsense. You would be mistaken. I do not find it in the least amusing that a document such as this should be proposed by Christian clergy to their congregations. On the contrary, I think it an alarming portent. In a time of growing anxiety great numbers of people still look to the Church for teaching, for reassurance and for guidance. In so far as they do so, it is because they think the Church has something to say to them, and something to give them, which cannot be had from any other source. All too often what they get instead is amateur politics and amateur economics, the sort of shallow silliness of which the Declaration on World Poverty is a quintessential example. As at other times in the Church's history, 'the hungry sheep look up and are not fed'. The clergy have authority or influence because they are the keepers and the expositors of certain truths and mysteries which countless human beings have found to be indispensable to their existence. They profane that authority and prostitute that influence when they put it at the service of fashionable propositions, political and economic, which they are no better placed than other men to understand or judge and on which Christians can reach opposite conclusions with equal fallibility and with equally good conscience. If the Declaration were an isolated incident, it could be ignored with the contempt it deserves. If, as I believe, it is a symptom, it would be wrong to keep silence, simply for fear of misunderstanding or offence.

5

MY COUNTRY, RIGHT OR WRONG

The Archbishop of Canterbury has been talking about patriotism and the slogan 'My country, right or wrong'. He is reported to have said that patriotism 'was a travesty if it was taken to mean "My country first, its wealth and demands first, to the neglect of the needs of other nations, including the third world" '.

I owe respect to Dr Coggan, as Archbishop of Canterbury, a respect which I gladly yield. I also owe him more than respect when he speaks with the voice of his Master, to tell me that the blessed are the poor, the hungry, the thirsty and the oppressed, and that a rich man —and presumably a nation of rich men—cannot by any contrivance enter into his Kingdom. But it is not with that voice that his Grace was speaking in the words I have just quoted. He was speaking the language of materialism and of bad elementary economics, and when he so speaks, it is the right and duty of a politician, with all due regard to human frailty and to the temptation, which we all are under, to fall into slovenly thinking and fashionable talking, to refute and to rebuke. I do so because the economic errors that the Archbishop—not for the first time— propagates are damaging to this nation and its people without in any way benefiting any other nation or people.

Let us then focus our attention on the Archbishop's

condemnation of 'putting the wealth and demands of our own country first, to the neglect of the needs of other nations'. There is one set of circumstances, and one only, in which that statement would not be nonsense—and that is if our country's wealth and the satisfaction of its people's economic demands were procured from other countries by forcible spoliation. In those circumstances, indeed, the process would be a curse to the taker and to the deprived. But of course that is not what his Grace had in mind at all. He was not thinking of Attila or Nadir Shah. He was thinking of the wealth which, collectively, a nation acquires by overseas trade and investment. In that context what he said is nonsense and dangerous nonsense, due to rudimentary misapprehension of the economic process.

It is not possible by way of trade for one partner to acquire wealth and satisfy his demands without the other partner securing an equal benefit. Trade is free exchange; and free exchange, by definition, can take place only when the transaction appears to the participants not only to advantage them but to advantage them more than any alternative course of action which they perceive. It is not less true when, on some supposedly common standard, one party is already richer than the other. Our trade with 'richer' America does not impoverish us while our trade with 'poorer' Russia or India enriches us; nor does the imaginary savage who receives beads and tobacco get less addition to his well-being than the trader who sails back home with nuggets of gold, not unless the trader gets out a machine gun and raids the village, a custom not now widely prevalent. It is one of the crudest errors to suppose that the so-called poorer trading partner is obliged by his poverty to trade and therefore gets a worse bargain. At the point of voluntary exchange there can be neither gainer nor loser, constrainer nor constrained. At the market price all are equals.

As the productive powers and the demands of the people of one country increase, their trade with the people of other countries shares with them more various and complex and abundant products: in the Archbishop's non-Christian terminology, it increases their 'wealth and demands'. Henry Ford enriched the inhabitants of Britain as well as those of Detroit; James Watt enriched the inhabitants of India as well as those of Birmingham. To complain that you would prefer villages without cars, or that gurus dislike railway travel, is simply changing the subject and observing that tastes differ and we all enjoy despising other people's. The Archbishop has it exactly wrong. By 'putting first our own wealth and demands', we do not 'neglect the needs of other nations' (whether in 'the third world' or not). We cannot help but multiply and satisfy more abundantly thereby the needs of other nations. There is no merit about it—our intentions are selfish—but the unintended results, judged by the archiepiscopal standard of material well-being, are beneficent.

It would hardly be worth the ungracious task of correcting elementary economic misconception, if that were all there was to it. But, as with most gross errors, there is a motive, whether conscious or not; and that motive is dangerous. It is to substitute compulsion for individual choice, and force for freedom. Those who tell individuals and nations that they are exploited by the processes of free exchange and investment do so to persuade them to take by violence and to give power to the wielders of force. That is why 'exploitation' is the synonym for commerce in the vocabulary of Communist imperialism. Where trade and its consequences are condemned, compulsion is inserted in their place.

The synod which Dr Coggan had addressed 'passed a motion calling on the government to increase its official overseas aid programme up to the level of 0·7 per cent of gross national product'.

I must not allow myself to be diverted into speculating whether it is more ridiculous or blasphemous for the General Synod of the Church of England to pass such a motion. The business is more serious. There is nothing here to do with charity, not even charity in the vulgar sense—let alone Christian charity. The Church is calling for the use of force—of force to extract resources from the people of this country, of force to determine the consumption, production and way of life of the people of other countries. It is seeking to supersede and denigrate the means by which the people of different countries confer material benefit in terms of their own respective values. It is poisoning the good conscience of an industrial and trading nation in the innocent and rational pursuit of admittedly material ends. If the spread of wealth and the satisfaction of material demands are to be the criteria, then British industry and commerce are to be criticized only to the extent that they fail to put their interest first.

The time has come, and is overdue, for a reaction against all manner of national and especially international institutions which, under the guise of benevolence, are in reality excuses for substituting compulsion for free will and diminishing the material benefit which human beings in different parts of the world ought to derive from freely pursuing by way of trade what they please to regard as their own best interests.

The International Monetary Fund and the World Bank, Unctad and development aid, the Common Market and its unpronounceable compacts with African and other states —all these are part of a grand 'conspiracy in restraint of trade', to use an old-fashioned legal term. They all depend upon hindering or stopping trade which would otherwise freely and lawfully take place. Anything that happens anywhere, like the raising of oil prices, is liable to be seized upon by power-hungry governments as yet another justification for multiplying those restraints and reinforcing that conspiracy. Scratch the surface of all such devices, and you discover below it the naked desire to dominate, to prevent the peoples of the world from voluntarily exchanging their goods and services to common advantage. Tyranny is never so dangerous as when it has donned the mask of beneficence. It is too bad if it is to wear the halo of Christianity as well.

6

THE PARADOX OF PERSONAL LIBERTY

My brief tells me that 'personal liberty as conceived in the modern West is a joint product of Greek philosophy, Roman law and the Judaeo-Christian faith, which provide imperatives for containing the tensions between personal claims and social claims, i.e., between personal liberty and the security of the community'.

It further informs me that 'present threats to both require the exercise of more power by legitimate authority and therefore the lessening of personal liberty'.

It finally asks me 'if this paradox can be resolved'.

I beg leave to question the two premises, and consequently the paradox in which they are alleged to result.

I do not believe that the personal liberties enjoyed under the laws and government of England owe anything either to Greek philosophy or to Roman law, though the vocabulary and mode in which we discuss them may do. I am not sure what is meant by the 'Judaeo-Christian faith'; but if it refers to the Christian Church and its Gospels and other teachings, I find, if anything, still less connection with modern western ideas of personal liberty.

On the contrary, though many of the strands in modern thought about individual freedom and liberty since the seventeenth century are deist, it seems to me that none is

Christian nor contains any room for Christianity. For example, it would be hard to imagine a more non-Christian assertion than the famous formulation of individualism in the second section of the American Declaration of Independence. If men are created with equal and inalienable rights to life, liberty and the pursuit of happiness and people make or unmake governments to secure the enjoyment of those rights, the incarnation, crucifixion and resurrection are supremely irrelevant. The universe of Christianity and man's place in it have no meeting-point with the Whiggish worlds of Locke or Bentham, libertarian or utilitarian. It is not that life or that liberty or that happiness which the good news of the Gospel announced to mankind. Nor is it only the Sermon on the Mount which assures us that the two sorts are mutually exclusive. From beginning to end the message of the Gospel is that we cannot have both; it has to be one or the other.

Without serious exaggeration one might assert that Christianity is not about individuals at all. Of course, as both perception and self-consciousness are the attribute of individuals, as only individuals can know or believe—the Creeds are (or used to be) in the first person *singular* for very good reason—there is a sense in which the individual is necessarily the basic unit of the Christian society as of any other human society, simply because, like all living creatures, men are born, live and die as individuals and, unlike all other living creatures, they are lighted as individuals by the peculiarly human λόγος (John 1.9). But in no other sense is society, Christian or any other, constituted or created out of individuals. It is nearer to the truth to say that society is the only human reality that we know, and that the individual is an abstraction in terms of which, for certain purposes, it is convenient or even

26

indispensable to think. Everything that is knowable or predicable about an individual—such as, for example, his liberty or freedom or rights or happiness—is derived from the society from which we have abstracted him in order to talk about him.

I am indeed asserting—and as a proposition which I would sustain apart from Christianity (say, in China or in 500 B.C.)—that there is no such thing as human rights or the rights of man. There can only be the rights—that is, the admitted claims of individuals against other individuals—which flow from the constitution and nature of a particular society. Human rights in the abstract, in abstraction from a given society, are an absurdity, a collection of sounds without meaning. You will see therefore why I could not accept the premiss in my brief that there are 'personal claims' and 'social claims', which law, philosophy or faith provides 'imperatives' for reconciling. In the end we can only describe societies, and part of the description may conveniently take the form of identifying claims which the nature of the various societies accords or accommodates on the part of the individuals comprised in them. This is how the Actons and the Leckys come to be writing histories of liberty; for taste or fashion may be gratified by arranging or classifying societies from the standpoint of the observer's own assumptions or habits of thought. More objectively, the classification can be considered as bearing upon the stability or durability or productivity (however identified) of the various societies. Always, however, we remain locked in a circular process: since the claims of the individual are derived from the society, there is no means of establishing a societyless or society-free vantage point.

When the Platonic Socrates in the *Republic* was asked to define a just man, he declined to do so unless he was first allowed to define a just society, or rather to construct a just society, for only within a just society could a just man exist. It was essentially the same assertion as I am here making of the relationship between the individual and society, except that Socrates started from the assumption that there was an objective or ideal justice, in accordance with which the just society could be modelled.

In relation to all the claims and values of the individual the Christian gospel effected a revolution or inversion— what Nietzsche, in another context, called a Revaluation of All Values. As I have said, the terms life, liberty, happiness are given not merely a different but an opposite meaning, and the concept of right or claim is itself inverted as grace and mercy. But the revalued values are still only apprehended and achieved by the individual through a society of which he is a part.

The Gospel is indeed a social gospel, though not in the sense in which that phrase is commonly used today to imply a gospel about secular society. The good news of the Gospel is imparted to the individual only as a member of a society, the same society which is both the kingdom of heaven and the group in the upper room to whom it is revealed that they are celebrating together the new Passover. The most fundamental heresy of all is to imagine that the Gospel is given to individuals or received by individuals or apprehended by individuals. Its inmost secret is that it is collective: divest it of that character, and it disappears while we as persons try to grasp it.

The classic description of the Christian society is St Paul's (1 Cor. 10.17), that 'we being many are one bread and one body, for we are all partakers of that one bread'. The individual is there placed in his true perspective as a corpuscle in the social body. He receives his nature from the nature of the body corporate, not vice versa. His life, his freedom, his happiness are derivative from his integration into that particular sort of society. A little earlier I was a trifle quizzical about the word 'Judaeo-Christian' in my brief. Perhaps I should not have been. The essence of Judaism was already collective: the salvation, the righteousness, the immortality which it offered the individual could only have by belonging, by partaking of a collective inheritance. As a member of a people chosen and redeemed he escaped from physical bondage, traversed the literal desert and entered the Promised Land across a geographical Jordan. When the nuclear explosion of the Gospel translated all this history into a language universal because no longer physical—with a sacramental Passover, a baptismal crossing of Jordan and the promised land of a 'kingdom not of this world'—it did not leave behind the collectivity of the Jewish people, but subjected it also to the same process of transformation.

It follows that I can only resolve the paradox as it was posed in my brief by removing one of the two terms. The fallacy of the paradox is that it treats 'personal claims' and 'personal liberty' as being co-ordinate with the other term of the paradox—'social claims' and 'the security of the community'. They are not, as the alleged paradox treats them, co-ordinates. On the contrary, the former is derivative from the latter; and this applies equally to all human societies and to the Christian society 'which is the mystical body of all faithful people'.

7

CHRISTIANITY AND SOCIAL ACTIVITY

Dialogue with Bryan Magee

MAGEE

Mr Powell, you are a Christian, and you are also a professional politician. What I want to discuss with you is the relationship between Christianity and political activity— or, if we want to speak more broadly, Christianity and social activity. The main position I want to put to you is this. When one reads the New Testament one sees that the greater part of Christ's mission consisted of what might nowadays be called good works: helping the poor, healing the sick, feeding the hungry and so on——

POWELL

And raising the dead.

MAGEE

—and raising the dead—that was one of them if you like! But unquestionably the things I have just listed constituted a great proportion of his activities; and a good deal of his teaching consisted of telling other people to go and do likewise. Today we live in a world in which half the people are so poor they don't even have enough to eat. It seems to me that if one is a Christian one must be seriously concerned to change this situation. Now, obviously, poverty on such a massive scale can be changed only by political activity. While the individual doctor or teacher who goes out to Africa or Asia to do something personal about it is hugely to be admired, individual effort like that is only a drop in the ocean. What is necessary for such a massive redistribution of wealth and power in the world as the facts require is large-scale political activity. And it seems to me that if individual Christians and the Christian Churches were really serious about what they say they believe, they would be committed to what one can only call the politics of welfare.

POWELL
To make the stones bread.

MAGEE
To make stones bread, if they could. But I don't find that the Churches are so committed. And it doesn't seem to me that you are so committed. If not, why not?

POWELL
My two interruptions, which you so tolerantly accepted, were, in a capsule, my response or retort. Let me take them in the reverse order. I metaphorically described the sort of programmes to which you were referring and in which you expected the Church, because it is the Church, to engage as turning the stones into bread—not a bad metaphor. But you remember the context is the invitation of the Devil to Christ at the beginning of his mission (Matt. 4.3; Luke 4.3). It was a temptation which he rejected. If there were any doubt about the point, it was followed by another invitation, to accept political office—'the kingdoms of the world'—to be the all-powerful ruler, who could bring justice and no doubt, in modern terms, economic growth by political power. The answer was: 'Get thee hence, Satan'

31

(Matt. 4.10). We all, when we read the Bible, read what we see or find there; but, you see, what I have found is the opposite to what you have read there.

Now may I take my other interruption? You said that Christ's mission was directed to the poor. Perhaps we will come back to the meaning in the New Testament of that word 'poor' on Christ's lips in a moment. But you instanced various healing actions: the opening of the eyes of the blind, the unstopping of the ears of the deaf, etc. Having noticed that, you omitted something else which Jesus did but which is not within the scope of the National Health Service—not even of our great teaching hospitals— the raising of the dead. What I am saying is that Christ's mission to the blind, the poor, the deaf and all the rest is only another part of his mission to raise the dead; that, as the raising of the dead is supernatural—is religious, if you like—so also is the rest of the healing mission of Christ, and that we are not imitating Christ, or fulfilling his commandments, when we are engaged in healing any more than when we are engaged in banking.

MAGEE

I wouldn't dream of denying—it would be absurd to deny—that a large part of Christ's mission was concerned with the supernatural. Presumably a Christian would believe that this was the most important part. But it seems to me as plain as a pikestaff that, on any natural reading of the New Testament, a great deal of it has to do with social activity. I'm not going to bombard you with texts—you could re-bombard me with a lot more than I could bombard you with—but let me just read to you what John the Baptist had to say to the people who came to listen to him (Luke 3.10–14). 'The people asked him, "Then what are we to do?" He replied, "The man with two shirts must share with him who has none, and anyone who has food must do the same." Among those who came to be baptized were tax-gatherers, and they said to him, "Master, what are we to do?" He told them, "Exact no more than the assessment." Soldiers on service also asked him, "And what of us?" To them he said, "No bullying; no blackmail; make do with your pay!".' Now that teaching is all *social*. He is talking to the army, he is talking to tax-gatherers, he is talking to people of all kinds and telling them how they should conduct themselves in their social relationships——

POWELL
John the Baptist.

MAGEE
—and what he is enjoining is in fact the redistribution of wealth. If you like, he is enjoining interference with the prevailing economic system in order to help the needy. That teaching is taken up by Christ on occasion after occasion. Indeed, we are told in the New Testament (Matt. 25.31 ff.) that when Christ comes in glory to judge us all, those who have given water to the thirsty, clothed the naked, fed the hungry and visited people in prison or the sick will go to heaven, while people who have not done these things will go to everlasting darkness. I don't say that this is all it's about—I wouldn't dream of saying that— but, surely, it's plainly *part* of what it's about. Christians have certainly believed so ever since.

POWELL
Well, now we have struck at an early stage upon a great difficulty, one which perhaps I feel more than many, because of my training not only as a classical scholar but also as a critic of texts. There are two ways of dealing with

this difficulty. One is that well-tried method of dealing with difficulties—to shut one's eyes to them. The other is to face them head on. Both methods have inconveniences. So let me once again try to divide my response to them into two parts, and take the textual criticism second.

I will say first, that it always seems to me that the central assertion or command of Christ is summed up in such words as 'Leave all, follow me'. That is not a command to be busy in the world. It is not a command, except amongst the brethren, to any form of social activity or political activity. It is a command to renounce. This is what the rich young man was told (Matt. 19.21): 'Sell all'—but then of course he would be left with the cash, so he had to get rid of that—'and give that away to the poor and'—finally— 'follow me'.

This is not an exhortation to a life of benevolence, of erecting and organizing lazar houses and old people's homes. On the contrary, Jesus told us to leave all that behind, because a man with possessions cannot enter the kingdom of heaven, which is only for those who not only have no possessions but have renounced mother and father and wife and children and brethren. So, my response on one level—as it were, the non-critical level—is that that to me (I can't escape it, I keep on hearing it) is what Christ said. Now, if I can have another moment or two at this stage——

MAGEE
You have a disconcerting way of making two points at once.

POWELL
That's not so bad as the well-known, triangular method of the interviewee, which is to answer the question, then deliver a well-aimed kick, and finally make a different

point which has to be dealt with at once. At least I'm not practising that device.

MAGEE

And you're not being subjected to it either.

POWELL

No, that's true; so we will maintain mutual harmony. However, the second approach is rendered unavoidable by your appeal to the well-trodden passage in Matthew 25 about the Day of Judgement. The key words are 'Inasmuch as ye have done it to the least of these my brethren'. Now, that's a mistranslation: it should be 'to these little ones, my brethren'. It does not mean 'Inasmuch as you succoured the poor or visited people in prison'; it means that 'Inasmuch as you helped my brethren, the so-called "little ones", it was done for me'. There's a perfectly plain technical meaning in the New Testament of the expression 'the little ones', which is made clear in this passage by the gloss, 'my brethren'. It means the disciples, in passage after passage, in which Christ says that as they are treated by the world, so he will regard himself as having been treated: 'It shall be more tolerable for Sodom and Gomorrah than for that city' (Matt. 10.15), 'it were better for that man that a millstone were hanged round his neck' (Matt. 18.6), etc. etc. In Matthew 25 these words of comfort to his disciples have been married with a picture of the Judgement where they don't belong, because after all where in that picture of the great Judgement are 'the least of these my brethren'? Are they in the gallery somewhere? So, you see, I can't help it: I just have to read, and ask about, what I see in front of me.

MAGEE

You've made two points . . .

POWELL

Yes, in connection with each other.

MAGEE

Two points in reply, then, also in connection with each other, and perhaps it would be a good thing after that if we could each put one point at a time. On your first point, you say that Christ's injunction to the young man who was rich—'sell all that thou hast, give to the poor, and follow me'—was not an injunction to endow hospitals, etc. or in any way be busy in the world. But surely you would not dream of denying that Christ himself was busy in the world? He simply *did* spend a great deal of time healing the sick, and so on——

POWELL

And raising the dead!

MAGEE

—all right, but you cannot just ignore what I am saying. The plain fact is—and I hope I don't have to keep repeating this—a lot of his mission was spent in healing the sick, feeding the hungry, consorting with and defending the poor, even defending prostitutes. He was down there in the depths of society, involving himself with social problems and actually doing something about them. And ever since then, Christians—at least, most Christians—have believed that being a Christian consisted in trying to be like Christ, and that that included trying to be like him in these respects. Now, this brings me to your second point. You say that when Christ spoke of those who fed the hungry, gave water to the thirsty, visited those in prison, and so on, he was talking only about those who did these things to his disciples . . .

POWELL
That's what he said.

MAGEE
Well again, the whole of Christendom for the last two thousand years has treated words uttered by Christ to his disciples as if they were uttered through them to us all. For example, at the Last Supper, Christ said to his disciples—

POWELL
'Do this'—

MAGEE
Yes. 'Do this. Eat this: this bread is my body; this wine is my blood', and so on. Christendom ever since has taken this as an injunction to all of us, not just to the people standing there at that particular time and place. It seems to me that if you were to extend the interpretation you gave of Matthew 25 to the whole New Testament, most of the New Testament would cease to have any relevance for us; it would become just a series of remarks addressed to whoever happened to be there at the time.

POWELL
But the passage in Matthew is not an injunction to the disciples as to how *they* are to behave. If it were, then I agree with you that there would be a perfect analogy with 'Do this in remembrance of me'.

However, you referred, if I may take one point out of your description of what you regard as Christ involving himself in social activity, to his having fed the hungry. Let us recall the occasion, which I suppose is in your mind, when Jesus fed the hungry; it was the feeding of the four or (variant) five thousand. How did he feed them? He didn't feed them by saying, Now what we need is agricultural development, we need more investment. He didn't feed them by saying, We must have a redistribution of wealth. How *did* he feed them? What does it mean? To me it means only one thing: the feeding of the five thousand is an evident allegory of the Mass, of the Holy Communion. He fed them with his body and blood. That is what the feeding of the five thousand is, and the point about it, as about all his other social activities as you call them, is that they are all deliberately and unmistakably miraculous or supernatural, which is significant surely. So, this is my reply to you, that Christ's feeding of the hungry was not a physical feeding but a supernatural feeding. It was not a feeding which can be imitated except by the imitation of Christ in the Church and in the Kingdom of God.

MAGEE

If you are going to say that all those things Christ is physically described as having done, he didn't actually, *physically*, do at all—that they are all metaphors—I can't go along with that. You can take the whole of the New Testament metaphorically, but . . .

POWELL

No, I am only inviting you to take literally what happened. If you take literally what happened at the feeding of the five thousand—I think a reading will suggest to most people that those who wrote those descriptions didn't mean it as a literal description, but never mind—you cannot mistake it for an example of how the hungry should be fed, how the general standard of living should be raised, how the undeveloped countries should be brought up to a level with the developed countries. It is obviously talking about something totally different, belonging to a different world.

MAGEE

But once you do take it literally—and you have now

38

agreed to do so—then you have to concede that Christ did spend a large part of his time doing good works in the natural and social worlds . . .

POWELL
No, no, no. If I take it literally, it is a miraculous intervention and breach of the natural world, it is the opposite of an invitation to reorganize the natural world in this way or that way for greater comfort, convenience, equality of possessions and so on. However you take it—if you take it as literally as possible or as allegorically (I don't accept the word 'metaphorically') as possible—in either case it is an irruption, it is a denial, it is a refutation, it is saying—if you like, in other words—the same sort of thing as 'Blessed are the poor, blessed are they that hunger'.

MAGEE
But you don't deny—and what's more you can't deny—that Christ did spend a lot of time healing the sick, and all those other things I keep mentioning ad nauseam. How do you explain it?

POWELL
But his healing of the sick, was it a social activity, or was it a supernatural activity? How did he heal the sick? He didn't heal the sick by the application of any practical, physical, social or medical method. It is perfectly clear in each case that the healing was brought about by faith or if you like—it is the equivalent—by a change of mind. This is perhaps expressed more drastically than elsewhere in the story of the centurion's servant or son, who was healed at a distance by the act of faith of the centurion. Surely there is nothing here about an activity of going around healing people to show how a community ought to be organized to look after its sick. It was a supernatural act which centred

upon a supernatural proposition—to believe, whatever be
the content of the belief, that Christ is Lord.

MAGEE

I don't think I can have made it clear what the point is that
I am making. We all know Christ is reported to have acted
in a supernatural manner, to have performed miracles, and
of course we all accept that this isn't supposed to mean
that we can all perform miracles just because he did. However, what his activities show throughout is a concern with
the underdog, the under-privileged, the handicapped. Over
and over again he says—not just in the one text I've
quoted but in text after text—'I have come to preach the
Gospel to the poor' (Matt. 11.5) or 'I have come to release
those in prison' (Luke 4.18). Now the point I am making
is, first, that if you are a serious Christian you should at
least *try* to share these concerns of Christ, and second, that
in the world we live in this means active concern with the
underdog, the poor, the under-privileged, the sick and so
on. And third, all this has radical political and social implications. This is the main point I am trying to put to you.

POWELL

And let me ask you, how did he release the prisoners?

MAGEE

Was he not able to strike their chains from them?

POWELL

I don't recall that event, but never mind. In what sense did
he, quoting Isaiah, say 'I came to proclaim liberty to the
captives' (Luke 4.18)? Not in the sense that Satan proposed to him, of teaching the doctrine of a national rising
or some movement to carry out a Howard penal reform
scheme? No. The prisoners, physically, to all appearance,
would remain in prison; but everything would be different

for them because of what Christ came to do. The poor would remain poor, the blind would remain physically blind; but their eyes would be opened and the ears of the deaf would be unstopped. You cannot either deduce from this activity of Christ a command to behave on a particular pattern in the world and with the materials of the world, or attribute a kind of social mission to Christ himself. In order to do so one must indeed stop one's eyes and ears.

MAGEE
In that case the early Christians stopped their eyes and ears. I am going to give you one more text, and then I promise I shan't do any more quoting. At least, I promise I shan't do any more reading. But I do want to read you this, because it shows that what the early Christians did was to interpret their mission in a part social sense. They practised what has since become a famous form of primitive communism. It says in the fourth chapter of Acts (vv. 32 ff.): 'Not a man of them claimed any of his possessions as his own, but everything was held in common, while the apostles bore witness with great power to the resurrection of the Lord Jesus. They were all held in esteem; for they had never a needy person among them, because all who had property in land or houses sold it, brought the proceeds of the sale, and laid the money at the feet of the apostles; it was then distributed to any who stood in need'. To *any*, you will note, not just among the apostles . . .

POWELL
Oh?

MAGEE
'To any who stood in need.'

POWELL
We won't quibble about that.

41

MAGEE

Are you going to say that the very first thing the early Christians did under the inspiration of Pentecost was to make a mistake, to get it all wrong and misunderstand what they took to be the social implications of Christ's teaching? For what I have just quoted shows that they unquestionably did think there were social implications—

POWELL

And they thought these were the implications for themselves as the brethren, the little group who were the inheritors—I don't think that is a theologically accurate word—to whom this thing had been given. They did indeed form themselves into such a society. At least our authority for supposing so is what is there described. But I must hear Christ, if I can, not in the centre of a tiny community in Judaea in the first century. He speaks to me and to all, and I must hear what he says; and I find nothing in that which makes the early Christian community in Judaea the pattern commanded and enjoined by the founder upon whom we believe. The entire history of the Christian Church is a commentary upon our endeavours to leap a gap between men who must needs live in an institution, as the disciples had to live in an institution, an institutional settlement, who must needs live in the world, cope with disease, sickness, misfortune, calamity, war—between all this and the absolute and supernatural commands and content of what Christ said and did. The whole history of the Church in all its aspects—all of them imperfect, partial attempts to reconcile what by its nature cannot perfectly and fully be reconciled—is the best commentary of all.

MAGEE

Well, I've given you examples first of John the Baptist, who came before Christ, then from Christ himself, and now from the early Church that came after Christ, and in all of them it seems to me his commands speak loud and clear. They speak loud and clear with social implications in a very plain sense, and were plainly understood as such by John the Baptist, the early Church, and most Christians ever since. Now I want to extend this point *ad hominem*. I'm directing a point against you now, though not in any unpleasant way. I think you will see what I mean. Listening to you, it seems to me that what you are doing is to be explained as follows. The social implications of the Christian Gospel are indeed clear, but they are of a kind which you cannot bring yourself to accept, because they conflict with everything you stand for in politics and social activity. Met with this situation you do not, as one might have expected, deal with it by saying, 'No, they don't have those social implications; they have others which are more in line with what I think'. With your characteristic unexpectedness you meet the situation by saying, 'They have no social implications at all'. And you then proceed to support this with perverse arguments. That, I'm afraid, is how it looks to me. But can you possibly *really* say that the injunctions of Christ don't have any implications *at all* for our social activity and for our political activity?

POWELL

If by implications you mean that one can derive from them—otherwise than by a process of self-deception—a preference for one form of political action over another, for instance a preference for a society organized on socialist lines over one organized on capitalist lines, I say 'Yes, undoubtedly, that is precisely what I am saying; there are no implications'. If, on the other hand, you say to me: 'Are there no implications for a man in believing that the Creator became incarnate and was slain and is alive for

evermore—statements so tremendous that the very pro-
nunciation of them is a limitation of them—do you say
that a man who has caught a glimpse of that is the same,
behaves the same, lives the same as a man who hasn't?'
then, of course, I reply, 'No, he must be somehow different'. But if you ask me, 'Now illustrate that from his
behaviour on the second reading of the Prices and Incomes
Bill next Monday'—which is a very big issue, a big issue
about the organization of society—I'm going to have to
reply, 'I'm terribly sorry, I can't'.

MAGEE
But we could easily pick an issue over which Christian
precepts . . .

POWELL
Try me on another issue then.

MAGEE
Well, for instance, if there were a number of homeless
families in your constituency, and the question came
before your local council—and involved you as the M.P.—
whether or not more public money should be spent on
housing them, it seems to me that you as a Christian would
have a clear Christian duty . . .

POWELL
Not at all. Two views can be taken upon the economic
cause and the economic cure—I'm using the word in the
widest sense so far as there is a cure at all—of homeless-
ness; and I do not see any reason why, because a man accepts
the central doctrines of Christianity, he would favour a
capitalist means of providing housing rather than a socialist means of providing housing, or vice versa.

MAGEE
Ah yes, but as long as he provides the housing.

44

CHRISTIANITY AND SOCIAL ACTIVITY

POWELL

Can I try to help? If his object in what he says—if my object in what I've said advocating market rents—I'll take you head on—were inspired by a hatred of my fellow-men, by a contempt for my fellow-men, by a desire that, so far as in me lay, I should render them more miserable than they would otherwise be, then that certainly could not be reconciled with a belief that Christ died for me and for them. I suppose one can just imagine that there are and have been people in politics whose activity is knowingly inspired by hatred, contempt; but it must be very unusual.

MAGEE

You have now introduced a whopping great Aunt Sally into the discussion . . .

POWELL

Have I?

MAGEE

Yes, because I haven't dreamt of suggesting that your political activity or anyone else's is motivated by—

POWELL

No. I'm trying to say that I find no relevant Christian duty unless you could get inside the man and say 'In choosing market rents rather than subsidized rents this man is not motivated by the belief that market rents by and large result in people being better housed than they would be under an alternative system'—which I do happen to believe, right or wrong—'but by ill-will towards his fellow human beings'.

MAGEE

But there is a clear Christian duty on the man who has, to give to the man who hasn't. And that is redistribution of wealth.

POWELL

How much? The Christian duty is to give all.

MAGEE

The man who hath substance should give of his substance.

POWELL

No, no, '*all* thou hast', if you're talking about Christian duty.

MAGEE

Even so, that's not the free working of a market economy.

POWELL

Nor is it the working of a socialist economy. However, thou hast appealed unto the early Christians, and they at least, like monks, had no personal property. If that is what you are talking about, then I come a little towards you. If you are saying that the command is irreconcilable with the economic world as we know it, because it enjoins upon everyone lack of possessions, lack of property, that he should leave all these things behind, then I agree with you. But then I ask how I am to jump that gulf which, wherever I look, I find the Church and Christ deliberately open up between the world and Christ?

MAGEE

You continually talk about this gulf, and you continually say it's impossible to jump it—

POWELL

Well, I would modify that, but go on for the moment—

MAGEE

I think this is to misunderstand the nature of standards. Let me take the example of truthfulness. Every single one of us in this world, in this life, has told lies, and no doubt

we'll all tell more lies; but we all acknowledge the importance of truthfulness as a standard. The fact that we are
not able to meet this standard absolutely doesn't mean
that it must therefore be held to have nothing whatever to
do with our behaviour. It's most important for us to be as
truthful as we can, and to come as near to the standard as
we can. I quoted to you the early Christians, who gave up
all their possessions. I quoted to you John the Baptist, who
had previously said, 'Let him that hath two shirts give to
him that hath none'. Now that was not following the
absolute standards of the early Church but was going half
way towards them. That's a very important thing to do.
All moral standards I think have this character. Whether
it's honesty, truthfulness, or whatever it may be, we are
unable as human beings to meet them absolutely; but the
fact that we are unable to meet them absolutely does not
mean that they therefore have no relevance to our daily
lives, or cannot be taken as guides to our daily lives.

POWELL

We are on a major point here certainly, a major issue and
once again—a gulf, because I do not believe that the commands and doctrines of Christ are standards in the sense
that the thirty mile speed limit, for example, is a standard.
We all break it sometimes, but nearly all of us would say
'It is right and we ought to comply with it'. But that is the
morality of the man who said (Luke 18.12) 'I give tithes of
all I possess'. He, you remember, got nowhere. He was
obeying, humanly speaking, the commandments of the law,
which cannot, as St Paul said, like any other law, be one
hundred per cent fulfilled. But the doing away of the law
by Christ was not the substitution for the ten commandments of a different set or the addition to them of an
eleventh. It was their abolition by an act on his part and by

the substitution of absolutes which are not attainable in the sense that it is possible not to commit adultery, not to commit murder, not to steal, not to bear false witness. For these he substituted other commandments which are different in character.

Now, you said—and it was a very fair paraphrase—that I had described this gulf as impossible to pass, and at that point I demurred. I make my correction now. It is a gulf between the natural and the supernatural, between the absolute and the human, between the inconceivable of the incarnation and the resurrection and the conceivable. That gulf is passed, I believe—and this is where belief comes into it for the first time—only within the Church, by the fulfilment of the command which you referred to earlier. It is only in the miracle, if you like, of the sacrament, the continuing repetition of the miracle of the Gospel, that the gulf is crossed. This is what the believer says—or tries to say, rather—to the agnostic.

MAGEE
Well, I can see that that may be part of the truth. But it seems to me plainly not the whole truth, because it is central to the whole spirit of Christianity that Christ was saying it's not enough to love God, not enough to say the right things, not enough to obey the law and keep religious commandments. You must do all these things, he says, but you must do yet more—you must love your neighbour.

POWELL
As yourself.

MAGEE
As yourself. But you must live a good life.

POWELL
No, he didn't say that . . .

48

MAGEE

And the living of a good life is central to what Christianity is about in its social context. You, I think, have placed yourself firmly on both horns of a dilemma—at least, on one or other of them . . .

POWELL

I'm not surprised—they exist!

MAGEE

You have a choice between the two following alternatives. Either what Christ said to us was meant to give standards which, though we cannot meet them absolutely, can nevertheless guide our behaviour. That is how most Christians have understood it. But you say they are wrong, that the standards are not of this kind. Or else you have to say that Christ told us to do a lot of things we can't possibly do. That seems to me to make nonsense of his mission on this earth, as a man in society.

POWELL

But he told us that these things can only be done, that the commands can only be fulfilled, are only fulfilled, by acceptance, in whatever sense that be meant, of what he is and of what he did. 'He that liveth and believeth on me shall never die. He that believeth on me though he were dead yet shall he live' (John 11.25, 26). The life that is offered, like the crucifixion and the resurrection themselves, is not a graduated response, a more or less successful fulfilment of standards put forward by the Master. It is the result of a quite different process.

MAGEE

What you are saying, Mr Powell, seems to me in effect, though not in intent, to lack compassion and magnanimity, and to leave out all those acts of giving that a

Christian ought to perform, not only on the personal level but on the political one. I want to relate this to something you were saying earlier. You talked about the indispensability of a Christian's finding the right place for his activity in the Church. It looks to me as if the Church is the wrong place. If you take a broad view of the world you could divide it up very roughly into a comparatively small number of people in Europe and North America who are white and well off, and a very much larger number of people in other places who are coloured and poor. The Christian Church is concentrated overwhelmingly among the well off. Now it seems to me that it ought to be keeping only a skeleton staff here and should be working in great force in Africa and Asia with its jacket off and its sleeves rolled up . . .

POWELL
Preaching the Gospel?

MAGEE
Yes, preaching the Gospel by word and deed—not only by word but by such deeds as feeding the starving, teaching the illiterate, healing the sick, and so on. A few Christians are. But the Churches as a whole are not.

POWELL
The preaching of the Gospel indeed is enjoined upon all Christian men; this is a command, like any other. But the healing of the sick and other activities, you remember how they were to be performed—it was to be done 'In my name'. That is to say, it is not an activity which is Christian apart from the Gospel itself. It is not a business of founding hospitals or teaching how to make two blades grow where one grew before . . .

MAGEE
But why not? Why not that way as well as other ways?

50

POWELL

Well, that's up to you; but you must not claim that it is part of the mission of the Church to improve agriculture in China or Africa, because, as I said, this is the very temptation of the Devil which was repudiated at the beginning of Christ's mission. This is the alternative, this is the—I use the word without offensive connotation—anti-Christian approach to the problems of the world, to the problems of man, to the problem of man. The Christian approach understands and teaches that if two blades grow where one grew before, if a hundred grow where one grew before, we shall still be as poor as we were before, we shall still be as blind and as deaf as we were before, without the Gospel.

MAGEE

Are you seriously saying that a Christian, *as a Christian*, has no particular obligation to the poor, the hungry, the under-privileged? Are you seriously saying that?

POWELL

I would need the meaning of obligation in that context to be defined.

MAGEE

What stops you giving me a straight 'Yes' as an answer?

POWELL

Most questions don't admit of 'Yes' as a straight and truthful answer. There was a Jewish obligation, a Jewish law, to give tithes of all that one possessed. There is an obligation under our law—secular law—to perform certain actions. But the obligation of Christianity is to give *all*. It is, like the other obligations of Christianity, an absolute; and I repeat, it brings me to the brink, as I listen and hear, of a gulf across which only the Church, across which only Christ himself, can carry me.

51

8

THE NOTION OF IMMORTALITY

A distinguished Canadian theologian began a recent book by saying that 'the notion of immortality does not occupy a central or even near-central position in much contemporary Christian thinking' and that 'the result has been to ignore one important dimension of the faith'.

I feel that this is true and I want to use the privilege which has been given me here in order to share with you some thoughts on that dimension.

I turn to Matthew 27.52–3.

> And the graves were opened; and many bodies of the saints which slept arose and came out of the graves after his resurrection and went into the holy city and appeared unto many.

Matthew's Gospel here describes one of the portents which marked the moment of Christ's expiry on the cross; not only was the veil of the temple rent from top to bottom; not only did an earthquake split the rocks; but the graves opened and their occupants walked abroad. This was one of the conventional 'perturbations of nature' which were supposed to signalize terrible human happenings. You remember from *Hamlet* how

A little ere the mightiest Julius fell
The graves stood tenantless and the sheeted dead
Did squeak and gibber in the Roman streets.

It was the sort of thing to be expected when an event occurred after which nothing would ever be the same again.

For a Christian, however, the passage presented an intolerable difficulty. The resurrection of our Lord, St Paul's 'first fruits of them that sleep' (1 Cor. 15.20), had not yet occurred. This was not the moment of his triumph and glory, but the very abyss and the nadir of despair. Yet here, as the lifeless body of the Saviour hung on the cross, was a whole crop of resurrections, flaunted openly in the streets of Jerusalem. The apparent slap in the face to a central article of Christian faith was the more palpable because the word used for the dead 'arising' was the same as the word for Christ's resurrection. There was also that deliberate emphasis on 'bodies'—the *bodies* of those that slept. This was no spectral hallucination, but a 'resurrection of the body'.

The passage occurs only in Matthew. Luke (who certainly used Matthew) and Mark (who scholars today are more inclined to believe also used Matthew) took the easy way out and simply ignored it. Still, there it stood in the text of Matthew, and somebody (we shall never know who) decided to take a knife to the Gordian knot. The dead, he concluded, must have been Christians, and their resurrection must have been after our Lord's. So he inserted the words 'the saints' and 'after his resurrection'. But alas, this solution was only obtained at the cost of a hopeless anachronism. These were portents which accompanied Christ's *death* and one of them could not just be held up for forty-eight hours or more. In any case, 'saints',

53

the early Church's expression for Christian believers, was about as appropriate at the moment of Christ's death as the word 'Anglicans' would have been.

Do not misunderstand me. It is far from my intention to poke fun at that earnest interpolator some eighteen or nineteen hundred years ago. When he struck upon this passage, he confronted a problem which confronts us too and perhaps, talking together across the centuries, he and we can help one another a little to live with it, though we shall no more solve it than he could. That we are so ready to duck the problem is no favourable indication of the seriousness of our faith.

When you once begin to look, you find that the Gospels are full of resurrections before Christ's resurrection. Jesus himself restores the dead to life before his Passion, starting from the 'ruler's daughter' and finishing with the raising of Lazarus on the last journey to Jerusalem. When the Baptist's disciples asked for evidence that the Messiah had indeed come, they were told that 'the dead are raised up' (Matt. 11.5). More strikingly still, when sending out his own disciples on mission, Jesus instructed them (Matt. 10.8) to 'raise the dead', sandwiched-in almost casually between 'healing the sick' and 'cleansing the lepers'. So, not merely did the raising from the dead not have to await the resurrection, but it could be performed in Jesus' name by others before the resurrection.

The difficulty is not disposed of by observing that an age with less medical knowledge was not aware of the abrupt physiological consequences of the break-down of the brain cells, and could therefore imagine that the possibility of resuscitation lasted much longer than it does, so that these miracles were to them no more than extensions of the 'kiss of life'. Certainly all those persons were raised to the life mortal, not the life immortal. The ruler's daughter and Lazarus would of course die again in due course like everybody else; their raising from the dead was only a deferment of natural death like any medical cure. But the resurrection to a *new* life was also taken for granted, by Jesus and others, before his own resurrection and independently of it.

The Sadducees' riddle about the seven brothers who married the same woman in succession is posed to Jesus with the question (Matt. 22.23 ff.): 'In the resurrection whose wife among the seven will she be?' The riddle is meaningless without a future life to which all are presumed to look forward; and Christ's reply: 'In the resurrection they neither marry nor are married but are like angels in heaven' presupposed a general resurrection Luke (20–34), like our old friend the interpolator in Matthew, found that intolerable, and therefore rewrote the passage so as to restrict the privilege of resurrection: 'The children of this world marry and are married; but those who are found worthy to obtain the other world and the resurrection from the dead neither marry nor are married, for they can die no more but they are as angels, and are sons of God, being sons of the resurrection'.

It was a bold and determined reinterpretation; but it left the underlying problem untouched. Was it not Luke (23.42, 43), no other, who added to the crucifixion narrative the contrast between the two robbers, with the plea: 'Lord, remember me when thou comest into thy kingdom', and the reply: 'Verily I say unto thee, today shalt thou be with me in paradise'—words which assert immortal life before Christ's resurrection and kingdom. After all, the essence of the Last Judgement scene in Matthew 25, with the sheep and goats, which was to fix the imagery of

Christendom for all time to come, was that resurrection to immortal life or immortal death would be universal and unconditional.

We know therefore what, in the view of the earliest narratives accessible to us, Christ's own resurrection did *not* mean: it did not confer either on his followers (in any sense of that term) or on mankind as a whole either immortality or participation in a final and general resurrection. If those existed, they existed independently of his resurrection. So we cannot run away. We stand in the presence of the question: what then *did* it mean?

Some of the highest Christian art has made it so much more difficult for us even to realize, let alone attempt to answer, that question. Nobody who has entered the gallery at Urbino and seen the masterpiece of Piero della Francesca, can ever forget the face of the triumphant Christ as he steps, banner in hand, out of the tomb over the prostrate legionaries. It is the subject of thousands upon thousands of less inspired representations. But the Gospel tells of no such thing. How much more logical, obvious and convincing it would have been if Jesus, in the face of men, visible, as he had been on the cross, and irrefutable, had smashed the tomb and come forth in victory! The unconscious yearning that this might have been so has inspired Christian art down the ages to represent it as having actually happened. But that was not what God chose to do, and not what the Gospel tells us that he chose to do.

The resurrection narrative, in the earliest form accessible to us, has already undergone considerable elaboration, but it is impossible to read that narrative without participating in a sense of bewilderment and even embarrassment, as if the women and the disciples suddenly found themselves in possession of something which they did not understand

and which they did not know what to do with. The Lord's crucified body was buried before nightfall the same day. There is then a gap. On the other side of that gap, there is no body but Jesus is already a living presence.

It is the gap between actions which are set in historical time and statements which defy time. The crucified body of Jesus could not be in the tomb because Jesus had already told his disciples what his crucified body was, and is. Indeed, the very word 'already', with its implication of before and after on a historical time-scale, mocks our comprehension. In timeless words, to which no tense of the verb, past, present or future, can be attached without falsifying them, he told his disciples that the body given for them is the bread broken, taken and eaten. The verb 'given' in that sentence is perfectly neutral as between past, present and future.

One of the greatest poets and thinkers of Christianity, so close to its beginning that we do not know his name, has left us an incomparable sermon on the resurrection. In Luke's Gospel the resurrection is signalized by two experiences. One (24.13–35) is the journey to Emmaüs, at the end of which the disciples recognized the Saviour 'in the breaking of the bread'; the other (24.36–43) is the appearance of Christ among the disciples to prove to them his bodily existence by eating the same food as themselves. Some time in the fourth century, or very likely earlier, words were added, which stand in the Latin text today, to the effect that after having himself eaten, Christ distributed the food to his disciples; but even without these words there would have been no doubt about the meaning.

Thus is crossed, if at all, the gulf between crucifixion and resurrection, which is the gulf between historical time and timelessness. It is the bridge which Christ himself made, and which *is* Christ himself. And thus we endeavour to answer, as the disciples did, the question: what is the meaning of the resurrection?

'And their eyes were opened and they knew him; and he vanished out of their sight.' (Luke 24.31).

9

THEN SHALL THE END COME

And then shall the end come.   Matt 24.14

When we read the New Testament we all do our own expurgation. Every individual no doubt has passages, even whole chapters, which he skips, and certainly every age has proceeded in this way with the Gospel. Among the parts of the Gospel which it is not merely common but positively good manners to tuck away out of sight in our own generation are those which deal with the end of the world and the second coming, the 'coming again with glory' which week by week in the Nicene creed we nevertheless assert to be an essential part of our faith.

There's no doubt about it: what is called 'eschatology', the doctrine of the end, is in exceedingly bad odour nowadays and most of us 'pass by on the other side', anxious not to be mistaken for the sort of people who in all ages have been convinced of contemporary identifications in the Book of Revelation or found infallible prophecies in the measurements of the Great Pyramid. If we are pressed into taking notice of the Gospel teaching about the end and the second coming, we are apt to explain that the whole thing was really a misunderstanding. Our Lord's disciples, under the influence of the ideas of their time, particularly Jewish ideas, supposed that the end of the world was imminent and interpreted accordingly what our Lord had to say to them. What is more, we are not averse from suggesting that the sack of Jerusalem by Titus in A.D. 70, which made a colossal impact on Jewry and through Jewry on the history of the Western world, has, as it were, infiltrated the Gospel, so that in this respect it is hopelessly 'dated'. As for us (the same line of defensive special pleading continues), with the immensely, inconceivably, wider time-scales that modern science has opened to us, we are entitled to treat the eschatology of the Bible merely as a product of its period, which we in our own day may permissibly ignore.

In any case, do we not know that astronomically this universe has aeons of time in hand? For modern man the end of the world can be relegated to the level of those rather tedious strip-cartoons which feature men with sandwich-boards announcing the imminence of that event. We know better, and must be careful as Christians not to make ourselves look ridiculous.

There is, however, a deeper and more dangerous reason for our refusal to take the gospel of the end seriously. It is because the modern non-Christian world has its own gospel, which is not only inconsistent with Christianity but repudiates it in so radical and absolute a manner that we feel obliged to stop our ears and pretend that we do not know what the Christian teaching really is. We are afraid otherwise to find ourselves out of the fashion—and that would never do! Is it not, we are told by bishops and archbishops, not to mention lesser fry—lay and clerical—essential for the Church to be 'relevant', which word is no more than a fashionable euphemism for 'fashionable'? This is akin to yet another motive; for often, when a doctrine of the Church is unfashionable, the reason for this is not that it is in conflict with other truth which we know or suspect, not because it has been disproved by modern science, but on the contrary because it is all too alarmingly scientific—in accordance, that is to say, with observed facts which we would fain suppress and replace by our own wish-fulfilment fantasies. And so it is with Christian teaching about the end.

Christianity does not, repeat not, look forward to a gradual betterment of human behaviour and society or to the progressive spread of peace and justice upon earth. Still less does Christianity purport to offer a scheme or general outline for bringing that about. Quite the reverse, it uniformly teaches, as if to emphasize the point for good measure, that things will get worse rather than better before we are through. So far from it being the function of the Gospel revelation to prevent that happening, the reversal which it promises is sudden, apocalyptic, external; something which irrupts into the world like a lightning flash.

This, like so much else that is Christian, represents a reinterpretation of the Jewish revelation so profound as to be a contradiction of it. The Jew looked forward—still does look forward—with the practical, earthbound, matter-of-factness characteristic of the Jew, to the actual establishment of his own theocracy in the world: swords *will* be beaten into ploughshares, and the kings of the earth *will* come bringing their tribute to the holy mountain of Sion, and everything will be splendidly organized for the best in the best of all possible worlds, under Jahveh's personal supervision.

The Christian is at once more humble and more realistic, and his hope is of a different sort. Christianity does not teach the improvability of human nature, individually or collectively; it teaches that its depravity is inherent and ineradicable. This is, to put it mildly, in no conflict with any facts produced by the sciences, which offer us no evidence to justify assuming the moral improvement, or improvability, of man. What it does conflict with are certain fashionable modes of thought and certain current political theories of comparatively recent date, which take unfounded optimistic assumptions about the perfectibility of man and human society as a basis for the acceptance of infallible prescriptions for perfecting them. It is consequently highly uncomfortable to be told by the Gospel exactly what we do not want to hear—so much so, that from the most authoritative ecclesiastical quarters there may often be heard proceeding words and sentiments which not only are not derived from the Gospel but actually repudiate it.

I have no wish to be unecumenical. Dear me, that would be too terribly unfashionable! Yet I cannot refrain from quoting the quite remarkable words which the Pope addressed to Harold Wilson on the occasion of the latter's recent visit to the Vatican. The Supreme Pontiff welcomed the accession of the United Kingdom to the European Economic Community—a provisional political arrangement, about which British electors are all entitled to hold their own opinion, and upon which I suppose the head of a foreign state may arguably be permitted to comment, though with due restraint. But what His Holiness said was astonishing:

> [In joining the Community] not only will Great Britain be furthering the cause of the brotherhood of all men but she will also be bringing closer the day when the goal of universal peace and justice will finally be attained.

Nothing could be plainer or more emphatic. If the actions of politicians, such as the governments party to the

Treaties of Rome and Brussels, can bring nearer the final establishment of peace and justice upon earth, then other similar actions can bring it nearer still and nearer, until eventually it must be attainable through their agency. You cannot both believe this and be a Christian; for if this is true, then Christ died in vain, and mankind can be saved and glorified by its own prudent endeavours. Whatever such a belief is, it is not Christianity; and surely it is a striking testimony to the compelling power of fashion that such language should be held, apparently without any sense of incongruity, by the successor of St Peter himself.

My argument has brought me to the brink of the familiar abyss. On what side then does the Christian range himself? Does he, or does he not, endeavour for his part, in his own person and so far as accords with his station and function in society, to oppose the evil and the foolish and the destructive in human nature? Is he for peace or war, for justice or injustice? Or does he contract out and wash his hands of the whole business? It is not because of the particular text I was unwise enough to choose that I find myself in this dilemma. I would have arrived there from any of a hundred starting points in the Gospel, by any of a hundred roads. Having got there, my ejaculation must be the same as St Paul's when he had argued himself to the same impasse (Rom. 3.31): 'God forbid!'

Christianity has not contracted me out of either human nature or human society, nor out of my place and endeavour in it. It has given me no promise, let alone assurance, indeed the contrary, of improvement, and consequently, and necessarily, it has given me no prescription for that. It has not authorized me to take one view rather than another of the likely outcome of introducing a large and growing alien element into a given society. It does not help me decide to vote for or against a United Kingdom in the European Community, or for or against the capital penalty for murder, or for a flat-rate or a graduated system of state pensions or, for that matter, for or against state pensions at all. Nor has it added to, or subtracted from, the moral imperatives of my society or of any human society, which serve the requirements of self-preservation and survival and would not themselves exist if they did not.

After all these negatives, the question then follows irrepressibly: 'Well then, if it does none of these things, what difference does Christianity make—to you or to a society of Christians?' The answer, as so often, perhaps invariably, with Christianity, is a paradox and a contradiction: nothing—and everything. May I go on quoting at one of these places where St Paul ejaculated 'God forbid!' (Gal. 6.14)?

God forbid that I should glory save in the cross of our Lord Jesus Christ, by whom the world is crucified unto me, and I unto the world.

The Christian is the individual to whom that is true, and to him the difference is nothing and everything: nothing that can be defined in terms of opinion or policy or judgement or decision; and yet everything, through thinking and judging and acting in the knowledge that men and human society, though not improvable, are redeemable, and that, in the way which only Christians know, their redemption has been performed and is available for ever.

10

WHERE DO WE GO FROM HERE?

A conviction that he is, or ought to be, or can be, in some sense immortal appears to have been part of man's make-up ever since he became man—by which I mean ever since he acquired that self-consciousness that makes him (so far as we know) unique.

The earliest that we know or can deduce about our race reveals us as essentially 'immortality-minded'. Perhaps one could fairly use a stronger term and say 'immortality-obsessed'. The total effort which man from his most primitive period has lavished upon providing for his immortality must greatly have exceeded that which he devoted to his accommodation and well-being in his pre-immortal span. The granaries of Egypt have not survived; her pyramids remain stupendous. In village and in city the houses which—until the most recent past, at least—have overtopped all the rest were the habitations of immortal beings, in whose immortality the builders believed they were able to share. Of his energies as a thinking creature man has bestowed—take him all in all—much the greatest part upon the world of invisibility and immortality.

It seems to me therefore that the most elementary, and not necessarily the least important, point to make is that concern with his immortality is part of man himself. He is an 'immortality-concerned animal', and he reveals himself as such no less powerfully in his agonizing attempts to be convinced that he cannot really be immortal after all, than in his most confident assumptions that he is.

In short, belief in immortality is an inseparable concomitant of human self-consciousness itself and, since our self-consciousness is an individual or personal self-consciousness, we are entitled straight away to insert the word 'personal' and say 'belief in personal immortality'.

Having advanced only thus far, we find ourselves at once locked in an argument in a circle from which there is no escape. The question, 'whether man is immortal', is replaced, as irrelevant or meaningless, by the question, 'in what manner man conceives his immortality'. In his endeavour to give form and substance to his innate belief man has perforce used the dimensions of which his consciousness and experience informed him, namely, space and time, which he has ransacked in order to find suitable lodging for his immortal self. As his knowledge of those dimensions developed, he pursued the search undaunted. For if, in the words of the Epistle to the Hebrews (11.14), man is one who 'seeks a country', it is a country he knows to exist before his exploration starts—like that writer's, his goal to which he travels, however distant or baffling, is predetermined.

So we have the voluminous geography of the spirit world, stretching from the nooks and crannies of the habitations of the living to the uttermost bounds of the universe. All man's powers of imagination and representation were taxed to describe that other world and to link it by a passable bridge or road system with this. To that vast library belong equally the Egyptian *Book of the Dead* and the eleventh book of Homer's *Odyssey*, essays characteristic of the spirit of the peoples who produced them.

Unfortunately this 'untravelled world' was one 'whose

66

margin fades for ever and for ever' as man moves. The Isles of the Blest had to be pushed farther and farther away as the bounds of the known mortal world extended, until eventually they were driven off the face of the earth altogether—and off its under-surface, too—into the skies, only to be pursued and eliminated there also by the growing resources and powers of 'man's unconquerable mind' in its other aspect, that of the ruthless investigator of physical fact.

But there beckoned another bridge from 'this mortality' to the world of immortality—the dimension of time. No wonder the other world could not be discovered here and now, for was it not 'the world to come'? The invocation of the magic of time offered to resolve impossibilities and absurdities: the Chinese princess covered with plaques of jade, the embalmed Pharaoh, the dry bones in the ancestor's tomb—they were dead, no doubt, dead as dead, but by the wand of the future tense, they would 'be made alive', either automatically and unconditionally or subject to certain necessary precautions having been observed.

This immortality, not now but some time, a sort of suspended animation, is the garment most familiar to western, Christian man, though the pagan philosophers of the ancient world knew it well in other forms. All futurist conceptions of immortality imply a world crisis, a decisive interruption at some point of time in the course of nature: the Last Judgement—the idea of 'last' is significant!—and the coming of Christ's Kingdom on earth; or alternatively the Stoic philosopher's *ecpyrosis* or burning-up of the whole universe, after which everything would start all over again, providing the immortality of the 'eternal repetition'. How ironical to recall that those words are the phrase of Nietzsche, whose defiant atheism could no more dispense with the conviction of immortality than the artless faith of the toilers in the fields!

The dimension of time proved more resistant to exploration than that of space. True, dates for the Second Coming or the End of the World had an inconvenient habit of proving premature. But this could be put down to impatience or miscalculation, and Carlyle could without misgiving assure the observer of those who lay buried in Ecclefechan churchyard 'in the expectation of a glorious resurrection' that, 'depend upon it, they have a long time to wait yet'. But alas, man discovered in the end how to sail the seas of time no less than those of space, and the horizon was as empty of the general resurrection as it had been of the Islands of the Blest. Temporally, as much as spatially, there was no breach in nature where man's conviction of his immortality could be located. So indeed, and with a different emphasis from the title of this talk, men might ask, 'where do we go from here?'

There was, however, another dimension, which I have not so far mentioned, in which man sought his immortality: the moral dimension. Man is a moral animal: the self-consciousness which made him man was also 'the knowledge of good and evil'. It was a moral being, knowing good and evil, as well as a self-conscious being, knowing himself immortal, to which the 'flaming sword' barred the way of return to Eden. The two ideas are intertwined, so that, to use the Christian terminology by way of example, the day of resurrection is also the Day of Judgement, and the eternity of the just is distinct from the eternity of the unjust. It would probably be impossible to point to any stage in the history of humanity when its ideas about immortality have been dissociated from its ideas about the rightness or wrongness of 'thought, word and deed' during mortal life.

WHERE DO WE GO FROM HERE?

The mode in which modern man conceives immortality must come to terms with what he knows, and cannot unknow, about the dimension of time. He can no longer understand it as a dimension which one day it is possible to 'walk out of'. Time is a manner of apprehending reality from which he has no means of escape and with which he has no means of dispensing; but he knows also that it is part of the description of himself. Time, it might be said, is 'in the eye of the beholder'. Man's claim to be, or conviction of being, immortal is therefore a statement about himself made in terms of time because no others are available to him; but it is not made exclusively in terms of time—as he might predicate the immortality of matter or of energy—it is also made in terms of good and evil, as thought, spoken and acted by a unique individual.

These are not necessities which Western man has confronted for the first time in the twentieth century. The expression of them, along with much else wholly or partly inconsistent with them, is part of his heritage. Those who bring the bodies of their dead for Christian burial are addressed with the words: 'He that believeth on me, though he were dead, yet shall he live; and he that liveth and believeth on me shall never die' (John 11.25, 26). It would be hard to formulate a more abrupt dissociation of the idea of immortality from the idea of time, or a more startling association of it with the content of the individual human mind. It is a state of conviction about man and about his relation with the world, about his nature and purpose—in short, about man and God—which is thus equated with his immortality itself. This mortal life is also the life immortal. It is not like some grotesquely diminutive antechamber to an infinitely vast hall, but is endowed—by what man thinks, says and does—with proportions and importance which we unsatisfactorily attempt to state in terms of time.

The question therefore 'where do we go from here?' is exactly and precisely the wrong question. We do not go from here, we *are* here; and the unique and solemn irrevocability of what we here are and do is asserted by mankind, as it has been since his emergence, by the conviction of immortality. The iron necessity of cause and effect, 'whatsoever a man soweth, that shall he also reap' (Gal. 6.7), is lifted thereby from the mechanical or trivial to the sublime. It is not abolished by that other conviction which man's moral nature links with his own immortality: that the universe from which he arose is itself moral. The Christian affirmation (John 3.16), 'God so loved the world that he gave his only begotten Son, to the end that whosoever believeth in him should not perish but have everlasting life', comes to us laden with the accents of generations past which have sought through one form and another to express man's twofold conviction, about himself and about the world. It shapes our thoughts and words and what we are; and we in our turn bequeath not indeed exactly what we received but what, through our thought and use, it has become.

'Everlasting life' is located neither in the spatial world nor in the temporal world. It is located in the moral world, that is, in the world where, because of his unique self-consciousness and therefore his unique sense of responsibility, man supposes himself to share the Creator's attributes of being 'beyond space and time'.

11

EASTER DAY

A tree in full blossom in spring produces an effect on the beholder that is not wholly pleasurable. The impression of intense beauty is followed instantly by a feeling of unease and even of dejection: it seems almost unfair that such an explosion of life, such a miracle of colour and joy, should take place and that we, the human spectators, are left unchanged and the course of our life still set irreversibly onwards to its end.

Ever since man was man—that is, ever since there was a being aware of individual birth and death—the sight of nature's renewal has stirred in him this feeling of estrangement, which is part of human self-consciousness itself. Man is *in* nature, and yet, because of his self-knowledge, not wholly *of* it. In the midst of it he feels an exile, doomed to the knowledge, and therefore to the reality, of individual extinction; not for him the repetition, the renewal, the immortality of the world around.

However, the self-consciousness which exiles man from nature has been accompanied from the beginning by a conviction that he too in his own fashion is somehow to be immortal. That is why in Genesis the fall of man—the consequence of his self-consciousness through eating the forbidden fruit—is followed at once by the promise of ultimate victory through 'the seed of this woman' (3.15). It is not an accident that in spring, when for unimaginable generations our ancestors have hailed the immortality of nature and sought ways to assert or procure their own, we celebrate the event which, mindful of Genesis, the apostle Paul described by saying (1 Cor. 15.22): 'As in Adam all die, even so in Christ shall all be made alive'.

But what *was* this Easter event from which innumerable millions have drawn the conviction that their individual existence has been placed outside the range and power of death? It is an event of which history has no knowledge. Our knowledge of it is derived only from and through a society of believers which is spread around the world and without which the history of mankind in the last two thousand years would have been unrecognizably different.

In the book which that society cherishes as its fundamental document, the event is recorded in four separate and partially contradictory accounts, of which only one even claims eyewitness authority. The accounts do not even make it precisely clear what the event itself was. The tomb in which a body had been laid was found empty. During the following weeks the person who had been dead appeared as living to those who had known him before death; but he lived no continuous ordinary life with them, and most of his appearances were not consistent with an ordinary physical body. After a short time the appearances ceased.

It seems so little for a central certitude about life and death to be founded upon. Yet that certitude has been founded on it, and this could not have happened unless the event itself had been outside the scope of history. Man's hope of immortality is not capable of being proved or disproved, fulfilled or disappointed, in history—that is, in the world of events in time and space. If it were, it would have happened and been done with long ago.

EASTER DAY

The expectation that we could be satisfied by history is a vain one; history would give us only a stone when bread was what we asked for. Just as vain is the expectation that a new and sudden certainty would have burst into the world like a meteor, carrying all before it and compelling the instantaneous assent of every witness: conviction has to be the inner confirmation of a hope and a necessity which existed before.

The announcement each Easter morning that 'Christ is risen' is neither the billionth performance of an old play nor an expression of feigned surprise at what the calendar and the church magazine have already 'leaked' to the public. It is a fresh assertion of the hope that is as old as man. It is fresh because what certainty we can have is in the present and not the past. Yet when we make it now, we gather up in our assertion all the elements of man's insight and aspiration which were inscrutably fused and unified forever two thousand years ago.

12

GOD SAVE THE QUEEN

The very words of the theme that has been allotted to me are of venerable antiquity and biblical authority. 'And Samuel said to all the people, See ye him whom the Lord hath chosen, that there is none like him among all the people? And all the people shouted and said, God save the king' (1 Sam. 10.24). Thence it comes that among innumerable other observances, those are the words by which the English for at least a thousand years have acknowledged their sovereign at the commencement of his coronation, and thereafter repeatedly as long as he lives.

The words might form the text for a discourse upon the merits of kingship in general or of ours, and of our present most gracious sovereign, in particular. But I was not, as I understand it, asked to stand here to deliver a speech on political organization, nor is the nave of St Lawrence Jewry being used for this gathering in default of a suitable lecture hall. I am bidden in a place of Christian worship, and because it is a place of Christian worship, to reflect with you upon the Christian meaning, if there is one, of those time-hallowed words.

In this church, as (except by default) in every other Anglican church throughout England, there are prominently displayed the royal arms. For a large number of Her Majesty's subjects in England *God save the Queen* is not only a prayer for the head of state, a prayer which they

74

pronounce in common with their fellow-subjects in the rest of the United Kingdom and throughout the world. It is also a prayer for the 'supreme governor' on earth of their Church. Through the exercise of the royal supremacy the belief of the Church of England is defined and its liturgy and forms of worship are fixed and regulated. These statements will still remain valid, albeit in a less direct sense than heretofore, even after the Acts of Uniformity have been repealed, if the House of Commons consents to do so—I hope that it will *not*[1]—by a Measure recently presented to Parliament. For the present, our creeds and our services are still authorized by the schedule to a statute of the realm.

This association of ideas, of secular authority with religious belief and observance, is one very indigestible to our time, and is in some danger of being brushed aside as an anachronistic irrelevance, quaint or offensive according to the point of view, but destined no doubt to be soon tidied away altogether. Surely the state, the power of the sword, the system of organized compulsion, can have no meeting-point with the inmost secrets of the heart or with words and actions which are meaningless unless they are (humanly speaking) unconstrained? It might indeed seem that from Elizabeth I to Elizabeth II there has been a continuous movement in one direction—from universal legal constraint and uniformity towards the elimination of all secular authority whatsoever.

If so, the impression is the result of looking at too small a part of the scene. When we enlarge our vision, we see not so much the steady onward movement of a single stream as the ebb and flow of a strong deep tide. Like body and soul in a human individual, the temporal and the spiritual, the secular and the ecclesiastical, are so twined together in

[1] It did: the Worship and Doctrine Measure, 1974.

religion that first one, then the other, seems to predominate in turn, because neither can exist without the other.

From the earliest form in which we can imagine it, the liturgy of the Christian church must have embodied somewhere a spoken and public declaration of faith. At that place there stands in our Anglican rite of Holy Communion, as in the Roman Mass from which it is derived, the creed which we commonly, though inaccurately, call the Nicene Creed. The authority by which it was established is an authority far older than the Parliament of our Tudor sovereigns. That authority was none other than the authority of the Roman emperors, the *imperium* itself. Constantine the Great was not baptised until he was dying. All his life, after as well as before the battle of the Milvian Bridge, he remained outside the Church; but it was his authority that made the Christian Church the church of the world, and it was his authority and the authority of his successors that placed upon it the stamp of unity and uniformity without which it could not be that 'catholic' or universal church in which the creed asserts that we believe.

As long as the Roman Empire endured, the emperor summoned the supreme councils of the Church. He presided or at least attended, in person or by commissioners; he paid the expenses, fixed the sessions, and decided the agenda; and finally he gave the force of law to the conclusions. As one historian has described it, the ecumenical councils were 'a means whereby the Church was ruled by a secular power'.

After the universal empire of Rome had been fragmented and transformed, it was not accidental that there followed for centuries an insoluble conflict between the authority of the tribal or national monarchs of Europe and the single authority which the catholicity of the Christian Church implied. Saint Thomas Becket and Saint Thomas

More were equally witnesses and victims of that conflict. Nor was it accidental that when in England the national authority decisively prevailed, under our Henry Tudor, he declared that 'this realm of England is an empire', meaning thereby another Rome, whose *imperium* could, and must, govern the Church so far as its imperial power extended. Finally, it was not accidental that the Protestant reformation itself, in the very act of attempting to get behind the imperial Church and start again from earlier back, invoked the secular power to authorize its work. Martin Luther understood this as well as Henry Tudor, if not better.

The national states which received the inheritance of Christianity from the Roman world, were, as the Roman empire had been, monarchical. The attribute of sovereignty was conferred upon an individual and the exercise of it flowed from an individual. In a monarchy the state's two faces, as both temporal and spiritual, present no insuperable paradox. The sovereign who receives authority from God exercises it under God. He is himself no abstraction or automaton, but a human being who shares with the humblest of his subjects the same faith, expects the same judgement and hopes for the same redemption. Indeed, a Christian monarchy cannot be a simply secular state, since neither the source nor the bearer of its authority is wholly secular.

When the English monarchy placed itself outside the jurisdiction of the papacy, it did not and could not divest itself of its spiritual character; on the contrary, it thereby asserted its spiritual character without compromise or abatement. It was not as a secular monarch but as an independent national monarch that Shakespeare's King John was declaring the mind of Elizabethan England when he said:

77

As we under God are supreme head,
So under him that great supremacy
Where we do reign we will alone uphold
Without the assistance of a mortal hand.

The English state was the only one which finally
resolved the great debate of the Middle Ages by the prin-
ciple of supremacy, that is, by refusing to recognize that
there could be any power or right of human compulsion
over its members which derived from a source outside the
realm, or that there could be concurrent sources of compulsion within the realm. This solution reflects, and no
doubt emphasizes, a characteristic of this nation which
differentiates it from other European nations on either side
of the Atlantic more than we or they commonly recognize.
On the European mainland and in America concurrence of
powers and limitation of sovereignty are taken for granted;
in Britain we simply do not imagine them. In every continental European state and in the United States of America
the ultimate sovereignty resides in a constitution, a written
instrument, and the power authoritatively to interpret it is
independent of, and therefore concurrent with, the exercise
of legislative and executive power. In the United Kingdom
the ultimate sovereignty resides in one person, upon whose
authority when in Parliament the law knows no limitations.

It is because everywhere else in Christendom the state
has been rebuilt within the last two hundred years upon
principles which derive sovereignty from elsewhere than
the monarch (even where the re-made constitution is in
form monarchical), that Britain is today the only surviving
state which exercises spiritual as well as temporal authority
and where sovereignty is ecclesiastical as well as secular.
This is not to say that elsewhere monarchs and chief magi-
strates are not members of the Christian Church. Of

78

course they are so. There may even be official recognition of one or more branches of the Christian Church for financial and other purposes. But the medieval dilemma of conflicting sovereignties has been resolved by secularizing the state and relegating spiritual authority to the private sphere. For us alone the identity of nation and Church survives in the symbolism of historical forms, and the link between spiritual and secular sovereignty is still, despite everything, a living reality.

I fear, however, you must feel that I asked myself one question but have answered—whether satisfactorily or not—a different one. I asked myself what was the Christian meaning of 'God save the Queen', and if indeed there *is* a Christian meaning. Instead I have talked about 'the link between spiritual and secular sovereignty' and 'the identity of nation and Church'—of all of which the Christian scriptures, let alone the Gospel itself, know nothing, indeed less than nothing.

'Fear God, honour the king' in the First Epistle General of St Peter (2.17), or St Paul's injunction (Rom. 13.1–4) to 'be subject unto the higher powers' because 'the power' 'is the minister of God', who 'beareth not the sword in vain', will get us nowhere. Those are admonitions that were addressed to a tiny religious community who 'confessed that they were strangers and pilgrims on the earth' (Heb. 11.13), advising them that it was not their duty therefore to revolt against the Roman world-empire. Good behaviour and passive obedience were to be their proper attitudes towards it.

The secret and the salvation with which that tiny religious community was entrusted lay in the most thorough-going repudiation that can be imagined of everything that makes a state or even a human society conceivable. The kingdom of its Saviour was not a reform nor even a transformation or perfection of any earthly condition; it was to supersede all human sovereignties and societies whatsoever. It was to do so here and now in the individual's heart and mind; it was to do so on the cosmic scale in the time-imagery of the Second Coming; and those who are curious to know the constitutional arrangements of Christ's kingdom will find them conveniently set out in the Apocalypse.

Now, 'God save the Queen' is not the passively indifferent ejaculation of such an unworldly or anti-worldly expectation. It is concerned with 'the kingdoms of this world'. It is the distinctive self-assertion, come what may, of one nation against the rest; she is not *their* Queen, she is *our* Queen, and her allegiance marks us off as a separate people. 'God save the Queen' is the explicit avowal, in the presence of the Almighty himself, of another obedience than God's, another banner than Christ's.

In Pushkin's *Boris Godunov* the priests approach the dying monarch in order to hold over his face, in the Orthodox fashion, the Gospel of salvation; but the Czar commands them to stand aloof until he has given charge of his kingdom to Feodor:

> Dearer thou art to me, my son,
> Than the salvation of my soul.

It is the authentic voice of the human animal. 'My immortality', it says, 'is the survival of my family, my throne, my tribe, my country. Let me but imagine that they will survive and, like Faust, I myself will go to eternal annihilation rejoicing.' With their sovereign or their fatherland in their minds, men in the hour of combat have invoked the God to whom Jesus prayed in Gethsemane and have offered a memorial of his sacrifice on Calvary. Under the title of the 'God of battles' they have appealed to him for courage in the presence of the enemy and made ready to fight in his name for a dynasty or an empire.

It is idle to deny it. There is a real paradox in all this, a real contradiction which it would not be difficult to see as blasphemous. 'God and my country'—how dare we say that we would offer our own lives and take the lives of others for a cause so strangely designated? The royal motto itself, *Dieu et mon droit*, 'God and my right', though adopted (so they say) by the pious monarch Henry VI, is an almost offensive collocation of eternity with vanity.

I do not believe that we shall resolve this paradox by denying one side or the other of the equation. Christianity does not offer the perfection or the abolition of human nature, either individual or collective. It was the old dispensation, not the new, which looked forward to the nation itself becoming a priesthood, to preside over a world of peace and piety. To man as a social animal, evolved with the instincts not only of personal but, stronger still, of collective self-preservation, the new dispensation offered an uncompromising demand of self-surrender, 'he that findeth his life shall lose it' (Matt. 10.39), and an unqualified assertion of individuality, 'except a man be born again, he cannot see the kindom of God' (John 3.3).

The essential Christian contradiction of the prayer 'God save the Queen' is not altered by rewriting the second and third verses: it remains, perhaps it is even more harsh, when we have eliminated

> O Lord our God, arise,
> Scatter her enemies
> And make them fall,

in order to make way for some more fashionably expressed sentiment. Rudyard Kipling saw further and deeper when, in *Recessional*, to the 'valiant dust that . . . guarding calls not thee to guard', he opposed not a national anthem to the 'Lord of our far-flung battle-line' but something of a different order altogether, the sacrifice offered by 'the humble and the contrite heart'; for only in the uniqueness and loneliness of the individual is it possible to offer, as we are commanded, the sacrifice of even that allegiance which we value more than our own life itself.

13

I BELIEVE

To say that you 'believe in God' means nothing; for you can give the sound 'God' any meaning you please. You must say *what* God. Very well, then, I believe in God the Father, God the Son, and God the Spirit, the Holy Trinity, which is the central affirmation of the orthodox Christian faith. Why?

In the first place because, living when and where I have done, I had the opportunity so to believe. If anyone says that this is an unfair advantage (or disadvantage), I reply that the universe knows nothing about equality of opportunity. The knowledge of other truths—gravitation, the molecular structure of matter, the conservation of energy—depends equally on the time and place of an individual's existence. Why not, then, the knowledge of even more important truth?

However, opportunity is not enough—opportunity must be taken. Whether we take our opportunities, and which opportunities we take or are capable of taking, does not depend on us. It is something which comes to us. If you like, it is something which is *given* to us. That is what Christianity calls grace. I can therefore do no more than describe how it has been given thus far to me—imperfectly, but nevertheless—to believe in God the Father, Son and Spirit.

This much is certain, that at some past time an animal

83

somehow acquired the power of thought and speech as we know it: the power to form ideas, to recall them at will, to arrange and connect them, and to communicate the result to his fellow animals by certain sounds. The Greeks, as usual, had a word for it. They called it *Logos*, whether you translate that word 'speech' or 'reason'.

Man—for he was that animal—discovered that in the Logos he had the key to the world around him: it gave him power over that world, the power of thought, if not the power of control. Often he got things wrong, misunderstood, imagined causes and reasons where they did not exist. He spent whole ages in the grip of what we now know to be gross errors. Still, to this day, as he penetrates inwards into the universe of his own body and mind or outwards into the universe of matter, time and space, he meets no boundary. Wherever the Logos takes him, there he finds it, as it were, awaiting him.

This can be accepted as reality or rejected as illusion. We cannot prove we are not living in a nightmare, where we argue only in circles, find only what we hide, see only ourselves, look nowhere but in our own internal mirror. Some even have suggested that each of us lives his own unique nightmare and that nothing exists except ourselves—you in your case, I in mine. It is an act of faith, no less, to believe that since nothing comes from nothing, that which became conscious in us as reason and speech, existed and exists in the world in reality, that the universe was always (so to speak) human from the beginning. By thus believing, we have already affirmed, with St John, that 'in the beginning was the word', that 'without it was not anything made that was made', and that 'the word became flesh and dwelt in us'. We may even go on to assert that 'the word was God', and so have a glimpse of God the Spirit, 'which lighteth every man that cometh into the world'. But why God the Father? Even more, why God the Son?

The animal which acquired reason broke loose thereby from the rest of creation. He ceased to be programmed, like other social animals, to behave in a fashion predetermined by the laws of evolution and survival. Being self-conscious, he was conscious of willing his own actions. Mistakenly or not, he believed himself free to behave in more ways than one. In short, he had the knowledge of good and evil, and could knowingly do evil—that is to say, sin. Now, if the Logos existed before it became conscious in mankind, so also good and evil—moral good and evil, not merely creation and destruction as physical processes—must have existed from the beginning. It was God, not Adam, who planted the tree of the knowledge of good and evil in the Garden of Eden. Moral good and evil are embedded in the universe itself.

Here, once more, we come to the edge of a gulf. We can shrug our shoulders and turn back; or we can try to go on across it. If so, we can only do it by faith, by believing; and what we must believe is that, though moral evil is as much of the nature of man and the universe as moral good, it can be overcome. The method is that with which mankind has experimented in infinite forms since the dawn of history. It is called sacrifice. But until two thousand years ago the essential ingredients were missing. The sacrifice has to be voluntary, and must therefore be self-sacrifice. The sacrifice has to be divine (since good and evil are both equally of God's creation), and must therefore be the self-sacrifice of God himself. So it follows that if the motive of self-sacrifice is what is called love, God loves the world, and sacrifices himself for it in conscious—that is, in human—form. He is God the Father and God the Son as well as God the Holy Spirit.

When we say that matters of faith cannot be proved, that is true; but it is not the important part of the truth. Of course faith does not belong to the realm of things that can be proved to reasonable satisfaction one way or the other. But faith is not believing what cannot be proved *because* it is unprovable. Faith is believing something which, though not provable, so takes possession of us that it is impossible afterwards to imagine living without it. It has the force of inevitability. If I am asked why I believe in the Trinity, I reply: 'Because it is inevitable'.

14

BIBLIOLATRY

The story of Gethsemane, or 'the agony in the garden', is found in all the first three Gospels between the Last Supper and the arrest of Jesus (Matt. 26.36–46; Mark 14.32–42; Luke 22.40–6). There are important differences between the three narratives, and each one of those differences is worth studying on its own account because of the insight which they can give into the growth of the Gospel; but that there is a central element, presumably the oldest, which is common to all three, is not open to doubt. It is roughly as follows. With the injunction to watch and pray, Jesus leaves Peter and two other disciples at a certain spot and goes some distance away from them. When he returns he finds them asleep; but the narrative tells us not only what he did but what he said in the meantime. He prostrated himself in prayer, and he said, 'Father, if it is possible, let this cup pass me by; nevertheless, not what I will but what thou wilt'.

Whoever first composed that central passage took great pains to make plain what sort of narrative he meant it to be. The words were uttered out of earshot of the closest disciples and in any case those disciples were by then asleep. Either trait by itself would have been sufficient to mark the intention, but both together are irresistible. Understood as history, there is no possible evidence for the crucial words of Jesus: the narrator has deliberately, and even superfluously, by the narrative itself removed the possibility of evidence. Short of the grotesque and almost blasphemous notion that on awaking the sleeping disciples, the Master said to them: 'By the way, I think I ought, for the record, to tell you what I have just said to my Father', there is no possibility of a source. The narrative and its truth is not that of history; it is that of poetry, of imagination.

Such passages are extremely rare in the Gospels. It is hard to think of many other acts or sayings of Jesus of which it is deliberately and expressly contrived that there should be no witnesses. The nearest parallel is perhaps the temptation in the wilderness, for which there are only two, equally unthinkable sources available—Jesus himself and Satan! The setting of the Gethsemane narrative is all the more remarkable because of the importance of the content: it is a unique expression of doubt on the part of Jesus as to the central necessity of the crucifixion as the essence of his mission. The words uttered on the cross in Mark and Matthew, 'My God, my God, why hast thou forsaken me?' are of a quite different stamp. Not only are they one of the elements of the crucifixion narrative, like the nailing and the division of the garments, which have been derived from the Psalms and particularly from Psalm 22; but they express an altogether different sort of doubt from the prayer in Gethsemane, which has no Old Testament precedent.

We are confronted therefore with an imperious question. Who was it that, in a form deliberately marked as imagination, introduced into the movement towards the climax of the Gospel, and of Christianity, this dramatic assertion both of Jesus' uncertainty and reluctance and also of his submission? And not only, *who* did it? but *when* did he do it? and above all, *why* did he do it?

I have made a strange beginning to an address to a diocesan men's society. You may think it even more strange when I add that I shall not answer my own questions. I do not know the answers and so far as I am aware, at present no one else does. By a process open to everybody here with no more equipment than a synoptic New Testament, a process which required (as it happened) no knowledge of Greek, let alone of Hebrew, I have led you to a sheer rock face with a locked door in it, and we have not the key to the door. It is as if, in conducting some scientific experiment or exploring some problem of physics, we found ourselves at an impasse; we have no means available to go further.

I shall return presently to that simile, but first let us notice what has happened to the familiar Gospels and their household words which have permeated common speech. They have suddenly become strange and mysterious; a third dimension of depth, and a fourth dimension of time, has been added to them. As we gaze, the hard polished surface of familiarity becomes a cloudy but transparent glass through which we peer down into depths where persons and things only partly discerned are moving about, twining together and then detaching themselves again.

It is a truism that Christianity is a historical religion. The truism is commonly understood in the sense that the credal events are marked against the calendar of history, of Tiberius Caesar and Pontius Pilate, of regnal years and radio-active carbon. But there is another sense too in which Christianity is historical. Its book—I am saying nothing about its rite—is the terminal state, or perhaps it would be a better metaphor to say, the open rock face, of a period of inner history, that dim pre-Gospel world into which we found ourselves staring in astonishment.

89

So strange and awe-inspiring is it, this glimpse of the four-dimensional Gospel, arising and growing in time, before and beyond our ken, that the first instinct is to turn and run, as fast as our legs will carry us, back home to the Bible that we thought we knew, plain, two-dimensional, consistent, inspired by the Holy Ghost and—true. That's it; above all, true.

Idolatry is a sin that nobody worries much about nowadays. We commonly assume that, like the smallpox or diphtheria, it has largely died out and is not likely, unless we resort to strained metaphor and talk about worshipping Mammon, to be a serious temptation to modern man. We have even, in these ecumenical days, given up accusing other sects, whom we happen to dislike, of indulging in it. Not so. Idolatry is as present a danger to modern man and to the modern Christian as it was to the audience whom the Old Testament prophets castigated for it. The sin of idolatry is the sin of taking the easy way out: something handy and comfortable to live with and to worship, which makes religion easy, manageable. Idols are not limited to the stocks and stones which Milton supposed that 'all our fathers worshipped'. Almost anything will do. The Gospels, for instance, Bible-worship, bibliolatry, the worshipping of a text (whether it be the Latin vulgate or the Greek *receptus*) is as idolatrous as the worshipping of the host. Both are a way of making it easy for ourselves, the substitution of a thing for the spirit, of an idol for the god.

The Gospels are indeed for the Christian, as the Coronation Service says of the Bible as a whole, 'the most valuable thing this world affords'; but they are not a possession to be made the object of idolatrous or superstitious worship. On the contrary, if we make an idol of them, they will not yield up to us the growing harvest of knowledge and insight and illumination that they have yielded to each successive generation of the Churches for some eighteen hundred years. They will do that only if we read them and question them with all the resources that the late twentieth century has at its command. In the middle of Victoria's reign many devout Christians feared, and would have prevented if they could, the advance of the new sciences of man and of the physical universe. They dreaded that science would get behind and beyond Christianity and disprove it. Their fears, we now know, were groundless. Below each depth which the sciences penetrated another depth has opened to receive them. In every direction, inwards and outwards, the macrocosm and the microcosm have disclosed only more and still more—another ocean beyond every horizon—and Christianity remains as little proved or disproved as on the day the *Origin of Species* was published.

It is as foolish to refuse to study the Gospels with the resources of the 1970s as it would be to refuse to study the world around us with the resources of the 1970s. I go further: there are no other resources that we dare use. A Christianity that was content with the knowledge, the method and the insight of past generations would be about as vital as a modern copy of the cathedral at Chartres. The men who shaped those statues and coloured those windows were expressing the utmost that they knew or conceived; they worked at the furthest margin of their comprehension, suppressing nothing, avoiding nothing. There is no other way. Modern man must wrestle no less strictly and fearlessly with Christianity in the twentieth century than his predecessors did in the thirteenth, and he must use his methods and insights as they used theirs. We shall find, if we do so, that the world in which we work is in as little danger of being exhausted as that of the sciences: we shall no more come to the end of the Gospels than science will come to the end of the universe. Every generation has to wrestle with the same stranger as Jacob: 'There wrestled a man with him until the breaking of the day. And he said, I will not let thee go, except thou bless me. And he blessed him there. And Jacob called the name of the place Peniel: "for I have seen God face to face" ' (Gen. 32.24–30).

It is unfashionable in this age to praise the Church of England. Doubtless it had, and has, great deficiencies; but at a time when all and sundry are busy devising ways to make Christianity relevant and modern, there is something which the Anglican Church has to say, and to say especially to us who are its children and its inheritors. It is a Church which not only has never despised sound learning but has never failed to find a place for the outcome of all earnest and conscientious study and research. When its members, therefore, ask amid the babel of voices, 'What are we to do, and what is to be our part?' the Church of England may well reply: 'Read the Bible, and above all, read the Gospel; and when you read, read as those who read for the first time, and read refusing nothing which the knowledge of your time can bring to your help'.

The Church in the twentieth century holds an unexplored treasure in its possession. What it has to say to the world of the twentieth century will surely be found there and surely has yet to be found. True, what it has to say will also be found in its rite; but the rite and the Gospel belong together more closely than the words and the music of a song, and the Church of England, as both Catholic and Protestant, asserts their co-equal inseparability. The student who explores the meaning of the Gospel explores the meaning of the Church militant.

Do not say: 'But this is too difficult; this requires effort for which we are not prepared, and knowledge with which we are not equipped'. One of the silliest and most dangerous fallacies about religion, and in particular about Christianity, is that it ought to be easy. In that respect 'the children of this world are wiser than the children of light' (Luke 16.8). What amateur, pursuing his hobby or playing his game, would not scorn the idea that it was, or ought to be, easy? On the contrary, be it never so trivial, he will try to find in it a depth and a complexity, even if they have to be imported. The very collectors of beermats, let alone the philatelists, would not thank you for making their business easy. We would not dream of approaching the exponents and researchers of the newest science, and say, 'Make it plain and simple for us'; in fact, we should be shocked and incredulous if they offered to do so. Yet when we come face to face with what has occupied two thousand years of mankind's history with its claim to be 'the way, the truth, the life', the stranger turns up with the insolent and foolish demand, 'You must make it easy for me, or I will not listen'; and all too many of us are ready to try to comply.

So when I say to you of the Church of England Men's Society 'Read the Gospel, and read with all the resources of learning and all the critical powers of your minds', refuse if you will; but at least do not refuse because what I ask is 'not easy'.

That, then, is what I have to offer; that, and no more. But as I began by reading, so I will finish by reading, so as to leave behind a thought, like a marker in the book.

The saying 'he that saveth his life shall lose it', which A. E. Housman once described as one of the greatest moral discoveries of mankind, occurs in no fewer than six passages of the four gospels as we have them. It is a statement sublime, awe-inspiring and complete in itself. It not only needs no addition or antithesis, it refuses one—there is nothing more to be said. Yet in all six occurrences, an antithesis follows it: 'he that loseth his life shall save it'. This belongs to a different world of thought: this statement, unlike the other, is not self-evidently true—not true at all without qualification—merely to lose one's life cannot be to save it. That is why John (12.25) altered the verbs and substituted (quite characteristically) 'love' for 'save' and 'hate' for 'lose'; 'he that loveth his life destroyeth it, and he that hateth his life in this world shall preserve it unto life eternal'.

However, simply to alter the verbs did not remove the difficulty. In order to give the second sentence any satisfactory meaning, the circumstances in which, or the cause for which, life lost is life saved had to be introduced. John, as we have just seen, did it one way, by giving it a moral and even ascetic flavour—hating one's life 'in this world'. A different method was adopted by the common source of all the other occurrences (Matt. 10.39; 16.26; Mark 8.35; Luke 9.24) except one (Luke 17.33). This was to insert the words 'for my sake': 'he that loseth his life for my sake shall save it' (or 'find it'). Thus firm ground is reached on the other side of the gulf which separates this statement from the starting point, 'he that saveth his life shall lose it'. We are in a different but a familiar world; a post-crucifixion, post-persecution, early Christian church world. Mortal life lost for Christ is eternal life gained. Even then, 'for my sake' seemed too bald. What did it mean: lose one's life because, or on behalf, of Christ? An editor of Mark felt this so strongly that he added 'and for the Gospel', words which, so to speak, extend the field of vision from Nero's Rome as far as the South Sea islands.

One last glance before we close the book. A single sentence has leapt an unbridgeable void between man's greatest and characteristically human moral discovery and the Christian promise of eternal life. When did it happen? How did it happen? Why did it happen?

94

15

THE FEEDING OF THE
FIVE THOUSAND

And when it was evening, his disciples came to him, saying,
This is a desert place, and the time is now past; send the
multitude away, that they may go into the villages, and buy
themselves victuals. But Jesus said unto them, They need
not depart; give ye them to eat.

MATT. 14.15

It is, of course, the beginning of the narrative of the feeding of the five thousand, in one of the two alternative
versions which appear, a chapter or two apart, both in
Matthew and in Mark.

A few weeks ago, *The Times* published a letter from a
distinguished public figure—not, as it happens, a
politician—who is also a devoted churchman, in which he
paraphrased these two verses. 'It was the disciples', he
wrote, 'who wanted to send the five thousand away after
the sermon, and Christ who insisted that they should be
fed.'

Now, that is precisely *not* the contrast in the Gospel.
Not at all. The disciples were equally anxious that the
people should not be hungry. Indeed, it was they who drew
the Master's attention to the problem in the first place. The
contrast in the Gospel is between two *methods* of providing

for the hungry. That of the disciples was economic—and incidentally quite a sensible economic method—they wanted the people to spread out and not force up the price by converging on the nearest village. The method of the Master was miraculous: he would feed them himself, and he gave instructions how it was to be done.

The contrast, I repeat, is not between unconcern and concern, nor between heartlessness and compassion; it is between the normal or mundane and the miraculous.

There are plenty of hints in the various versions of this miracle to suggest to us what it means. The time was towards eventide, just the hour at which occurred the miracle in the house at Emmaüs, when the risen Christ broke the bread and in so doing was recognized by the disciples. More pertinently still, the people (according to one version) had been foodless in the desert for three days. It is the desert which stretches from Good Friday to Easter Sunday, from crucifixion to resurrection, from this age to the Second Coming. The miracle of the 5,000 is the miracle which will take place again here in a few minutes time, when our priest, the successor of the disciples, obeys the same instruction, 'give ye them to eat'; and sure enough the bread, which has fed countless millions already and is feeding them today, will prove sufficient, and far more than sufficient, to feed you and me.

Now, the reason why I quoted the letter from *The Times* was not in order to score off the writer, nor to emphasize the extreme importance of reading what the Gospel actually says and not what we imagine it says. I quoted it because the writer went on as follows: 'Christians may fall short of the ideal set by Christ, but at least we have a standard which we try to follow'. Doubtless that is true— the 'imitation of Christ' was a pervasive Christian theme ages before the German mystic wrote his famous book under that title—but all the more must we be sure what it is that we are to imitate.

If we are to follow 'the ideal set by Christ' in the story of the five thousand, we are not invited to set about organizing improved production and distribution of food: that was what the disciples proposed, and were forbidden. We are invited instead to do what Jesus did, namely to perform a miracle, and the miracle which he did, and does, is nothing less than to feed others with his own body. If we mean seriously what we are saying when we talk about imitating Christ, it is his being crucified and nothing less— for that is the basis of the miracle—which we are called to imitate.

We have much to learn in this matter from the Middle Ages. Medieval man was quick to associate being slain with working miracles. Thomas of Canterbury was as pig-headed a politician as even an Angevin king might hope not to encounter. But from the moment when he was killed without resistance, his body began to work miracles, and his glorified figure shone down from the windows of many a parish church—until Henry VIII found the case of another Thomas, Thomas More, too close for comfort and had them all smashed. Yet not before he had made that other Thomas too into a saint—by executing him. It was not even necessary that the victim be an archbishop or a scholar. Edward II was no paragon of the virtues, and his involuntary death at Berkeley Castle was more horrible than heroic. Yet his tortured corpse was sufficient to raise the glorious Perpendicular gothic of Gloucester choir by the miracles which it performed.

This is not some far-fetched, fanciful paradox to which we find ourselves led by linking the miracle of the five thousand with the injunction to imitate Christ. On the contrary, our conclusion, however dismaying, is writ large across the face of the Gospel. Whenever in the Gospel Christ says—either to a particular person or to men in general—'follow me', he makes no secret and leaves no doubt about what the signpost on the road along which he is to be followed says. It is marked quite clearly: 'To Calvary'. In order to follow him, we are to 'take up our cross', which can only mean that we too are to go along the *Via Dolorosa*. It is our 'marked route'. When St Paul spoke of being 'crucified with Christ', he was not merely making an abstruse theological statement about the doctrine of redemption by vicarious sacrifice. Little though we may like it, he meant what he said, and the tradition of the Church has insisted that he and the other disciples were in fact put to death, lest we be left under any misapprehension as to what it is that the disciple has to learn from the example of Christ.

Of course, as the letter in *The Times* put it, we shall 'fall short of the ideal'. The miracle which the feeding of the five thousand symbolizes was produced through an act of self-sacrifice destined by its very definition to be unique. That does not alter the fact that for us also suffering is the supreme form of action. More changes are wrought, and greater miracles performed, by what men allow others to do to them than by anything that they do to others.

16

THE WOMAN TAKEN IN ADULTERY

The story of 'the woman taken in adultery' is one of the famous Gospel stories, though it comes only in St John's Gospel (8.1–18) and perhaps—I shall come to this later—not even there. It has given us a proverbial saying, 'Let him that is without sin among you cast the first stone', which is used by millions who have no idea where it comes from. The story has been a great favourite with artists, especially the French romantic and biblical painters of the last century, who revelled in the contrasting attitudes of Jesus writing in the dust, the scribes and Pharisees wondering what to do next, and the woman pathetically, but seductively, displaying her ample charms.

So we imagine we know the story and that we don't need to read it again or think about it. If anyone asks us what happened, we reply without hesitation that Jesus told the priests they were as bad as the woman if the truth were known, and so he shamed them into letting her go. It reminds us of nothing so much as a master who, instead of giving the offending schoolboy six of the best, good-humouredly tells him to be off and not do it again. It's all very cosy and, between you and me, just a bit corny. There must be something wrong; for Jesus was not a cosy person who went around doing corny acts. Of that we may be sure; for cosy people who go around doing and saying corny things don't get themselves crucified.

So perhaps we had better look again. If we do, we shall find the narrative anything but cosy.

First of all, the woman is guilty: it is carefully emphasized that she was taken in the act. So apparently the only question is of proceeding to judgement and punishment. That the legal punishment is death by stoning our Lord does not query. Instead, he makes an astonishing statement: 'Let him that is without sin among you cast the first stone'. The proverbial familiarity of the words will prevent us, if we are not careful, from taking in how remarkable and puzzling the statement is.

One thing is clear, however unwelcome, to those who like to think of Jesus laying down precepts for practical application in society. The proposition that only the sinless can punish the guilty, if it is to be acted upon, would put an instant end to all laws, courts, prisons: the entire apparatus of law and its enforcement would dissolve. The consciousness of his own sinfulness cannot possibly, and should not, restrain the judge, the policeman, the warder and (if the law includes the capital penalty) the executioner from doing his duty.

There is no escape by way of pretending that Jesus was criticizing only the barbarity of the punishment. If the penalty were electrocution or corporal punishment or imprisonment or a stiff fine, the point would still be the same: 'Let him that is without sin among you set about applying the law'. Our Lord is evidently not talking about penal reform at all. In that context his words make nonsense. So what *is* he talking about? Agog, we read on.

One by one the court and bystanders turn away, until Jesus and the woman are left alone. 'Doth none of these condemn thee?' he asks her, and she replies, 'None'. The remarkable word there is 'condemn'. Jesus does not ask, as one would have expected, 'Is none of them prepared to cast the first stone?' Instead, for the punishment he has substituted the verdict—'condemn'; and yet we know from the start what the verdict had to be—it was a formality, for she was 'taken in the act'. Why the sudden switch from punishment to judicial finding? It cannot be accidental.

But now follows a sentence like a lightning flash: 'Neither do I condemn thee'. What? Our Lord himself, by definition sinless, will not even judge, let alone punish? So not only can a sinful judge or executioner not condemn or punish. Christ himself declines the office: 'neither do I condemn thee'. Who then *does* condemn and punish? That is the question. Jesus is not saying, as we would fain read the passage, 'Well, considering all the temptations, the respective ages of your husband and yourself, the hour of night and the fact that you had had rather too much to drink, I can hardly blame you—though mind, unlike those other bounders, I've never sown wild oats myself. I propose therefore simply to bind you over for a couple of years'. The words 'Neither do I condemn thee' have no more to do with mitigation of sentence than the previous words had to do with penal reform.

Who does, then, condemn and punish? As we ponder the question in the instant of suspense which follows the lightning, the thunder overtakes us: 'Go; and sin no more'. We have indeed left the world of police, of courts, of judges; they have 'gone out one by one, beginning from the eldest even unto the last'. The woman is alone, alone with the eternal judge, who declining judgement, pronounces instead a more piercing sentence: 'Go, and sin no more'. It is as impossible to the woman as to the scribes and

Pharisees, and she knows it. She has pronounced her condemnation upon herself, not only for the past but for the
future, in the light of the unfulfillable injunction held up to
her like a mirror. Judgement and punishment and all the
machinery of society as it goes about its law-keeping and
law-enforcing business are as far away as another contin-
ent.

Very often our Lord's words do not reveal their full
meaning until they are understood as ironical; and it would
be far better to understand the sentence 'Go and sin no
more' as a bitter irony than to substitute in its place, what
Jesus does *not* say, 'Run along, and try to behave better in
future'. But there is always in the irony of Jesus a depth
and a compassion which ordinary irony does not have.
Was it not himself who by his own death would solve the
insoluble problem and relieve the intolerable sentence
which he compelled the woman taken in adultery to pronounce upon herself?

If we have found this story difficult and the lesson hard,
we are surely not the first to do so. Possibly in your Bibles
the passage is printed in small type or between square
brackets. The reason is this. There are two main streams
into which the Greek manuscripts of the New Testament
divided even before the oldest copies that we have; and it is
only in one of those two streams that this story is found.
Did somebody miss it out; or did somebody put it in? My
own hunch is that the story is authentic, and that someone
somewhere left it out because he found it too difficult.
'This will never do,' thought he; 'how can the law be kept
if only the sinless can execute it? and what shall we come to
if adulteresses are to be let off with a warning?' So out the
passage came.

Christ from his own day to ours is misunderstood and
misheard far more often than not. You have to listen hard

to hear exactly what he is saying; you need to think hard about it and above all, you need to open your heart as well as your eyes and mind. Well does the psalm say to us at every Morning Prayer: 'Today if ye will hear his voice, harden not your hearts'.

17

THE GOD WHO HIDES HIMSELF

Jesus said unto them, Verily, verily, I say unto you, 'Before Abraham was, I am'. Then took they up stones to cast at him: but Jesus hid himself and went out of the temple going through the midst of them.

John 8.59

'Jesus hid himself'—the words are haunting. Jesus is indeed the god who hides himself, who, when we try to come to physical, human terms with him, 'hides himself and goes out of the temple through the midst of us'. Even as we stare into his lineaments, they fade and disappear; yet, a moment after, he is somehow there again, inescapable—the god who hides himself at the same time as he is *Theos Epiphanes*, the god made manifest.

During Holy Week, from one side of the world to the other, mankind will be looking at Jesus on the cross— surely a sight as plain as plain can be. But what is the spectacle that we are watching? Anxiously we turn again to the familiar words of the Gospel, which takes us as near to the scene as we can come, but yet not very near. The Gospel that for some reason is called after Matthew is basic to the rest. But even Matthew is already very old before it comes into our view. It is like some geological formation where the layers of superimposed rock tell the story of one epoch after another that came and went, each leaving their deposit. The work of many hands, the thought of many minds, has gone to make what we call Matthew.

'And after they had crucified him . . .' (Matt. 27.35)— the critical event has already happened before it is related—what happens then? 'They' (presumably the soldiers) 'parted his garments, casting lots.' It is the first of three quotations from Psalm 22, which form the framework of the scene: 'they part my garments among them, and cast lots upon my vesture'. The second quotation is the mockery of the passers-by, 'all they that see me', said the psalmist, 'shake the head, saying, He trusted in the Lord; let him deliver him, seeing that he delighted in him'. Finally, there are Christ's own words, the first verse of the same psalm: 'My God, my God, why hast thou forsaken me?' Well might a Jew actually so cry out in his death agony; but how came the Roman soldiers and the bystanders to be miming the very same psalm?

Psalm 22 contains another striking verse: 'they pierced my hands and my feet'. There is no mention in the Gospels of Jesus being nailed to the cross; the nails make their appearance only incidentally in the apparition of Christ in the narrative of 'doubting Thomas' in John (20.25). But the verse of the psalm may have been one at least of the reasons which led, many centuries later, to Christ beginning to be depicted nailed hand and foot, with arms extended. A strong tradition which runs through Christian art since at least the fourteenth century represents the two thieves as crucified not in the unique manner associated with Jesus, but in more anatomically plausible postures with their arms bound over the cross-bar. So the cross itself, the instrument of redemption, the manifestation of Christ 'lifted up' to 'draw all men after him', is wrapped in an unfathomed mystery.

In the Matthew narrative as it has reached us the elaboration on the themes provided by Psalm 22 had already been taken still further by the use of another psalm, Psalm 69. To the Hebrew invocation *Eli, Eli* ('my God, my God') had attached itself the punning or ignorant comment of the mocking bystanders: 'This fellow calleth for Elias; let us see if Elias will come to save him'. Something quite separate, however, has intruded between the two sentences spoken by the bystanders, showing that it is of later origin. This is the man who 'ran and took a sponge and filled it with vinegar and put it on a reed and gave him to drink'. The key is in Psalm 69: 'They gave me gall for my meat; and in my thirst they gave me vinegar to drink'. Hence came also the passage where immediately before the crucifixion, 'they gave him vinegar to drink mingled with gall'.

So as we look more and more closely at the scene of the actual crucifixion, the central, self-sacrificial act of God which is at the heart of Christianity, the more it is withdrawn from our eyes behind veil after veil of scriptural allusion and poetical elaboration. Jesus has hidden himself and gone out of the temple through the midst.

Perhaps no one more movingly described our bewilderment, or more convincingly reassured us, than the great but unknown poet who composed the resurrection narrative in the last chapter of the Gospel called Luke's. Two disciples on the road are joined by Jesus, but, as the narrative says, 'their eyes were holden, that they should not know him'. A long discourse followed, in which the stranger provided a new interpretation of the Messianic promises throughout Jewish history to show that it was indeed Jesus who had 'redeemed Israel'. Then comes the moment which never fails to stir the emotion, when 'he made as though he would have gone further, but they constrained him saying, Abide with us'. It leads to the climax when the stranger 'took bread and blessed it and brake and gave it to them'. Only then 'were their eyes opened and they knew him'. For an instant the veil was lifted; but only for an instant. The words immediately follow 'and he vanished out of their sight'. Once again Jesus had hidden himself and gone out of the temple through the midst. As the two disciples reported to their fellows, 'he was known of them in the breaking of bread', a moment in time, and yet it was his answer to their vehement desire, 'Abide with us'. He had not refused their plea; he had fulfilled it, but in his own way, elusive yet inescapable.

18

THE ARCHAEOLOGY OF MATTHEW

One of the most remarkable and important facts about Christianity is that it has four Gospels; but that fact has been so familiar and integral from a fairly primitive stage in its history that we have the greatest difficulty in looking at the Gospels without preconceptions blinding or distorting our vision. One such preconception is that the Gospels are witnesses in their own right to certain events, that they are directly or indirectly 'sources'. The most trenchant German criticism of the Gospels, dismembering them into component parts of diverse origin, building up genealogical trees of the various materials used by different Gospels in different ways, has still not broken the spell of the 'four Gospel-makers'.

This spell has prevented the consistent and unprejudiced application of the most basic of all the tests of criticism, the question *utrum ex utro*, which from which? The answer to that question determines not only an order of time but an order of dependence. It is a question which, unlike most of the questions of criticism, can often be answered with complete objective certainty. It is also a question which avoids the obstacles that editing, or corruption, or conflation place in the way of most methods of critical investigation. Its application transforms the study of the synoptic Gospels, and enables the evolution of the

Gospel itself, and thus something of the history of the Church, to be studied in depth with new material; for existing material in a new light is the equivalent of new material.

I will begin with a simple illustration, and move on to more complex ones. In doing so I shall use the familiar names Matthew, Mark and Luke to denote the respective Gospels in their earliest known form, but without any implication of unitary authorship, still less, of course, of any connection with the personages whose names have been assigned to these texts.

It is now recognized that the original form of the famous comparison with 'the lilies of the field' in Matthew (6.28) was: 'consider the lilies of the field, how they card not neither do they spin'. Through several stages, which I need not describe in detail, this was corrupted into the meaningless text which we know: 'consider the lilies of the field, how they grow, they toil not neither do they spin'. The corruption started through the word 'grow' being substituted for 'card not', with which in Greek it is nearly identical. All our existing texts of Matthew have the familiar corrupt text, except—and it is an exciting exception—that 'card not' has been erased underneath 'grow' in the fourth century *Sinaiticus* which is the earliest surviving complete New Testament manuscript. The known fragments of papyri which are earlier do not happen to cover the particular passage.

Now, in Luke 12.27, the only other gospel which has the simile, the corresponding sentence is 'consider the lilies of the field, how they spin not neither do they weave'. Clearly of the two alternatives, 'card not, neither do they spin' and 'spin not, neither do they weave', the former is the original. 'Spin not neither do they weave' could not be corrupted into 'card not neither do they spin', but 'card not neither do they spin' could, and did, produce 'spin not, neither do they weave'—and we know how: it was corrupted into the form we have in Matthew, and then a good but not brilliant piece of critical editing put it back into sense, on the analogy of the parallel simile of the fowls of the air, by deleting the meaningless 'how they grow, they toil not' and providing 'spin' with its natural fellow 'weave'. Only the corrupt text in Matthew explains how 'card not neither do they spin' became 'spin not, neither do they weave' in Luke.

We know therefore that, in this passage at any rate, Luke was using, and critically and constructively editing, the text of Matthew, then already deeply corrupted, which our earliest MSS preserve. He had no other MS which contained the uncorrupted text, though a trace of it still existed elsewhere as late as the fourth century.

In itself the deduction is of immense significance, in that it establishes to that extent the dependence of Luke on Matthew and the freedom with which he used him; but the consequences do not stop there. We are compelled to ask if the same conclusion applies generally. If so, we stand face to face with the question whether Matthew was Luke's *only* source, or at least his only source in the nature of a Gospel story. In other words, is there anything in Luke which cannot be accounted for as derived from Matthew or devised by Luke himself? Is there anything which necessitates the assumption of another source?

If the answer is no, then the evolution of the Gospel takes on a dramatically new aspect. Its earlier stages can be known only through excavation of the textual strata in Matthew, on top of which were erected, as if before our eyes, the structure of Luke and—I now add, as I turn to my next example—of Mark!

After the arrest of Jesus in Gethsemane, Matthew

(26.58; 69, 70)[1] relates that 'Peter followed after him at a distance as far as the court of the highpriest, and going inside sat down with the servants to see the outcome. And a serving maid approached him saying, "Thou too wast with Jesus the Galilean".' Now let us read the same event in Luke (22.54–6): 'They took him [Jesus] into the high priest's house; and Peter followed at a distance. They then lit a fire in the middle of the court and sat down together and Peter sat amongst them. Then a serving maid saw him as he sat in the firelight and, looking closely at him said: "This fellow too was with him".' It is an imaginative and vivid enhancement of Matthew and furnishes an explanation for Peter being recognized among the crowd although it was night. From Luke now turn to Mark (64.54)[2]: 'And Peter followed him at a distance right into the highpriest's court, and was seated with the servants and warming himself in the light; and one of the highpriest's serving maids came and seeing Peter warming himself looked at him and said, "Thou too was with Jesus the Nazarene".'

This passage not merely suggests but proves that Mark was using Luke, because while using him he has misunderstood him. He liked the touch about the fire which Luke introduced, but missed the point of it, and so described Peter as 'warming himself' which is irrelevant. The significance of the fire is not that it warmed Peter but that it lit up his features and enabled him to be recognized. This also explains the inappropriate use by Mark of 'light' ($\varphi\tilde{\omega}\varsigma$) instead of 'fire' ($\pi\tilde{o}\rho$): it comes from Luke's 'as he sat in the light', that is, the firelight.

What is more, the passage illuminates Mark's manner of

[1] I have omitted the verses 59–68, the trial in the sanhedrin, which interrupt the narrative and are (significantly) an intrusion into it. Luke, who perceived this, shifted it to a later point.

[2] I have, as in Matthew omitted the intrusive passage of the sanhedrin trial and joined up the two separated parts of the narrative. See above.

working. He followed Matthew basically, which is why, in this instance, he has the trial in the sanhedrin at the intrusive point where it occurs in Matthew and not in the place to which Luke has editorially removed it; but he had Luke beside him and drew from him details and touches which took his fancy.

Thus we can provisionally establish the basic relationship as follows:

St Augustine recognized long ago [1] that Mark was a copyist and abbreviator. The reason why his true position in the tradition has been so consistently mistaken is the impression of 'primitiveness' which he gives, due particularly to two features—the abrupt commencement, without any genealogy or birth narrative whatsoever, and his great brevity compared with the other Gospels. In fact these are not evidences of relative antiquity.

To anyone 'not defending a thesis', as Aristotle would say, it is obvious that the end of Mark in its original form has been lost. The narrative simply could not conclude with the words 'they told no one anything, because they were afraid'—a statement in itself illogical because incomplete—and without any appearance at all of the risen Christ. Various manuscript families contain alternative supplements drawn from the other Gospels or freely composed. Therefore the end of the archetype had been torn off and lost before it became the parent of all the manuscripts which we possess. Exactly the same had happened at the

[1] *De Consensu evangelistarum, i.2(4).*

beginning of the book, leaving the text to start in the middle of a sentence with the words 'as is written in Isaiah the prophet'. Over this was then inserted the title-heading, 'Here begins the Gospel of Jesus Christ', now absorbed into the text as the beginning of the first sentence. So the Mark which we have is mutilated at beginning and end, and originally contained a nativity (whether Matthew-style or Luke-style we cannot know) as well as resurrection and ascension. We can go further and deduce that the copy thus mutilated was not a roll (which had only one end vulnerable) but a codex (which can lose both covers). The mutilation of course occurred before Mark was combined in the one volume with Matthew, Luke and other writings, which incidentally indicates that the codex form of book was already in use by then.

As for Mark's brevity, it is the brevity of the epitomizer, not the primitive. Read, for example, the passage in Mark which follows the baptism in Jordan (1.13): 'And straightaway the spirit drove him out into the desert. And he was in the desert forty days being tempted by Satan, and was with the beasts, and the angels ministered to him'. No human being would understand what all that was about without knowing the narrative in Matthew. The omission of Matthew's temptation dialogues, ending with the words 'Then the devil left him', has deprived the phrase 'and the angels ministered to him' of its significance. Mark has cut the passage fearfully, and made little amends by the would-be literary touch, 'with the wild beasts'.

The three synoptic Gospels are thus documents of very different character. In the text of Matthew, as we have it, is laid down the evolution and elaboration of the Gospel story from the earliest point at which it becomes visible to us to the form in which it was taken in hand and deliberately carried further by Luke and then epitomized by Mark with the assistance of the work that Luke had done. The purpose and the philosophy, not to mention the other literature, with which Luke worked, are of absorbing interest: we can follow step by step his reflections and decisions as he read with scrupulous and analytical care what was before him in the text of Matthew. It is not beyond possibility that we could eventually identify his environment and make some approximation to his date. For the moment I do not want to follow that line, but to return to Matthew and, archaeologically speaking, dig a trench or two to expose the strata.

Matthew commences with three separate items: the genealogy from Abraham; the virgin birth; and the visit of the magi, introducing the flight into Egypt and return to Judaea. This last block is itself the product of several stages of elaboration on a basic narrative which motivated the sojourn in Egypt. Immediately afterwards there is a false transition (3.1): 'in those days appeared John, the Baptist'. The transition is false because the immediately preceding sentence is about the settlement in Nazareth following the death of Herod, 4 B.C. But the subsequent mentions of John are to be marked by much severer difficulties.

Jesus arrived at Jordan and is baptized and acknowledged by the voice from heaven. After this he goes into the wilderness; but the temptation which follows (4.1) does not fit. 'Then Jesus was led away into the desert by the Spirit, to be tempted by the devil; and when he had fasted forty days and forty nights he afterwards felt hungry.' This is the prelude to the three temptations by Satan. However, the word 'afterwards' is not merely superfluous but

114

grotesque. Jesus ought to have been hungry during the forty days and the temptations ought to have taken place in the course of them, as indeed the temptations of the Israelites in the wilderness, on which they are modelled, took place during their forty years. The sense required is simply 'and he went hungry forty days and forty nights'.

Then quite suddenly, there follows after the end of the temptations: 'And when Jesus heard that John was taken' (or 'betrayed'—it is the same word as is applied to Jesus himself at the crucifixion) 'he returned to Galilee'. These words must have originally followed a passage which described and gave reasons for the arrest and imprisonment of the Baptist, a passage which has been suppressed and then or later replaced by the forty days and the temptations whereas the original sojourn of Jesus in the desert must have been much longer, and terminated not, as now, by the completion of the temptations, but by the news which summons Jesus to take up John's mission where it was broken off and in the identical form: 'from then began Jesus to proclaim and say, Repent, for the Kingdom of Heaven has drawn near' (4.17 repeats 3.2).

The next main block, after the calling of Peter and Andrew, is that long collection of sayings called the Sermon on the Mount, which runs through three long chapters (5–7), which Luke broke up and distributed over the narrative, providing dramatic settings or introductions for the separate sayings. Then, after a series of healings and miracles (8–9.34), follows a further, shorter block of exhortations and sayings, addressed on this occasion to 'his twelve disciples' (10.1), now mentioned for the first time, whose names are then given (10.2–4), beginning with Peter and Andrew and ending with 'Judas Iscariot, which also betrayed him'—a touch which identifies the reference to the twelve and the nominal list as a later addition.

It is after this that, without transition, there comes (11.2) the second reference to the Baptist: 'And when John heard *in the prison* the works of Christ, he sent by his disciples and said to him' etc. The words 'in the prison' show that the deleted passage about John had described his imprisonment. Jesus' reply to the enquiry which, incidentally, is quite inconsistent with John's recognition of Jesus at the baptism, and his discourse on John as the forerunner, shade off into further teachings and 'works' (11.20–13.58), until there comes, once again quite suddenly and unexplained, the third and last reference to the Baptist: 'At that point of time' (which?) 'Herod the tetrarch heard the report of Jesus, and said to his sons, This is John the Baptist, he has risen from the dead, and that is why the power to work miracles is in him'.

Quite apart from the fact that Herod had no sons, it is an astonishing statement: John has evidently died without our being told. Moreover, to Herod the miracles of Jesus only begin after John's death, not after his arrest and imprisonment—and are only explicable on the basis that Jesus is John raised from the dead.

It is true that the sentence is followed by an explanatory passage (14.3–12), which relates the arrest and imprisonment of John by Herod, and his decapitation at the request of Herod's step-daughter; but the passage is betrayed as a later and uncomfortable addition by its conclusion: 'And his disciples came and removed the corpse and buried it, and went and reported it to Jesus. And when Jesus heard, he departed from them in a boat to a desert place alone'. The transition is absurd; for the narrative of John's death begins as a 'flashback', whereas at the end it is treated as a chronological part of the narrative.

Amid much that our excavation has left uncertain, what is clear is that in an earlier form of the narrative, John played a much more important part, which has been deliberately as far as possible obliterated. The effect of the obliteration has been, again deliberately, to give the impression that John survived during at least the earlier part of Jesus' mission but to maintain between them the relationship of forerunner and Messiah and the effective termination of John's mission before that of Jesus commenced. What could be the motive for this drastic remoulding?

The only known reference outside Christian literature to John the Baptist is in Josephus, *Antiquities*, 18, 5, 2 (116–9), written about A.D. 93. Josephus states that during a visit to Rome, Herod agreed to marry Herodias, the wife of one of his half-brothers (also called Herod), and to divorce his existing wife whose father was Aretas, the king of Petra. Unbeknown, news of this reached the wronged wife in advance, and when, on his return from Rome, Herod allowed her to go to the frontier fortress of Machaerus, she promptly absconded thence to her father, who sent an expedition which, with the help of traitorous elements, destroyed Herod's army. On receipt of this news, the emperor Tiberius ordered Vitellius, governor of Syria, to attack Aretas and either bring him alive in bonds or send his head. Vitellius took two legions and had reached Jerusalem on his way south when the news of Tiberius' death in March, A.D. 37 reached him and caused the operation to be called off.

Into the middle of this narrative, between Tiberius' order and Vitellius' departure, Josephus inserts a self-contained section, to the effect that 'certain of the Jews believed that Herod's army had been destroyed as a just vengeance for John called the Baptist, whom Herod had killed. He was a good man, who told the Jews to practise virtue, be just to one another and pious towards God, if they came for baptism—because only then would the baptism be acceptable to God, being sought not as an atonement for sins but as a purification of the body after the soul had already been cleansed by righteousness. His words aroused great enthusiasm and crowds gathered. Herod therefore, fearing that John's influence with the people, who seemed ready to do whatever he advised, might end in insurrection, thought it much better to kill him first before any mischief resulted than to regret his failure to do so when a revolt had occurred and he had trouble on his hands. So on Herod's suspicion John was arrested and sent to Machaerus, "the aforesaid fortress", where he was put to death.'

There is nothing in common between this and the account of John's fate in Matthew; but on the basis of Josephus' narrative the Baptist's death would have occurred about A.D. 36, and Josephus says nothing to suggest a lengthy previous imprisonment. On this chronology, if Christ's ministry had not begun until after John's arrest, there would be little or no time for it, if Christ was to be crucified under Pontius Pilate; for Vitellius dismissed Pontius Pilate from his procuratorship right at the end of A.D. 36 and sent him to Rome, where he did not arrive until after Tiberius' death the following March.

If the narrative of the Baptist in Matthew before the commencement of Jesus' mission originally included the account of his arrest and death, the chronological difficulty would be intolerable. The only way to lessen it was to maximize the interval between John's arrest and his death by removing the account of John's death and substituting the vague word 'betrayed' for 'killed'. The impression of a long imprisonment is then sustained by the message from John 'in the prison'; and finally, when the Baptist's death

118

has at last to be narrated, it is treated as if contemporary with an advanced stage of Christ's ministry, despite the context ('Can John the Baptist have risen from the dead?') which pushed it into the past.

All this difficulty only arose if it had to be by Pontius Pilate that Jesus was condemned to death. Why this necessity for the dating by Pontius Pilate? What I believe may be the answer is suggested by the temptation narrative, which, as we have seen, has been inserted where a passage about John's demise originally stood. The forty days of Jesus in the wilderness are the re-enactment of Israel's forty years and began, like them, after a sojourn in Egypt. More important, the forty years began with the liberation from bondage at the Passover, by the blood of the Paschal lamb. If Jesus, 'the very Paschal lamb', redeemed Israel with his blood, Israel still had before it forty years in the wilderness before reaching the promised land. The drama was enacted first in a miniature scale: the absolution by baptism and the forty days. The second enactment will be on the grand scale: the absolution is by sacrificial blood; the period will be forty years; and the Promised Land is—what?

After the capture of Jerusalem and the destruction of the Temple, orthodox Jews throughout the world ceased to celebrate the Passover with the liberating blood of the lamb; for were they not again in bondage and the Temple, where alone the lamb could be killed, destroyed? If, however, the course of Jewish history were reinterpreted, the destruction of the Temple was not utter calamity and rejection, but the inauguration by fire of a new age of universal salvation: through it the new promised land, the Messiah's kingdom, was reached and entered. If so, the true Passover, the sacrifice of the 'lamb of God', could be positively dated. It had taken place forty years before A.D.

70—in A.D. 30, upon which date the validity of the new drama of salvation depended. The Roman governor who was to be God's instrument, as Titus was to be his instrument forty years later, must therefore be Pontius Pilate, whose governorship ran from A.D. 26 to A.D. 36.

If we follow the train of reasoning, the decisive stages in the evolution of the Gospel—indeed, in the rise of Christianity—take place after the fall of Jerusalem and because of the fall of Jerusalem among a Jewish community which might have been anywhere in the Roman world. It might indeed have been in Rome itself. Certainly the earliest form of Matthew bears the traces of having been explained for users whose native language was not Greek.

The earliest known external references to Christians occur in the second decade of the second century, when Pliny the Younger as governor of Bithynia obtained the Emperor Trajan's instructions on how to deal with the recalcitrance of a sect who were called Christians. About this same time Tacitus and Suetonius—who were acquainted with one another and with Pliny—identified as Christians some of those whom Nero executed for complicity in the fire of Rome in A.D. 64. This, the sole external ground for dating Christianity before the fall of Jerusalem, rests on the assumption that Tacitus had a direct source—there is no contemporary evidence at all—and had not merely concluded that, since Christ 'suffered under Pontius Pilate' according to the Christians, the sect which was causing trouble just at the time when he wrote must already have been among those whose outlandishness and unpopularity made them suitable victims for Nero.

There was ample time between A.D. 70 and the early part of the second century for the evolution of the Gospel as we know it in Matthew, and for the church of which this was the book to have begun to come to the notice of the secular authorities.

We have travelled a long way from the lilies of the field; and yet I have offered only a small specimen of the riches that the textual treasure-house known as Matthew has hardly begun to yield to unbiassed critical analysis.

19

THE FORBIDDEN TREE

I am allowing myself the luxury of not just one text, but two. The first is Isaiah 45.7: 'I form the light, and create darkness; I make peace, and create evil; I the Lord do all these things'. The other text is much more familiar. It is from Genesis 2.9: 'And out of the ground made the Lord God to grow . . . the tree of knowledge of good and evil'.

If a single proof were required that indeed 'salvation is of the Jews' (John 4.22) and that our inheritance of Christianity is from a people who were uniquely 'chosen', it would be the unswerving and unalterable monotheism of the Jews which is expressed in these two statements from the law and the prophets.

Alone of the peoples around them, however much they borrowed from their neighbours' mythology and traditions—indeed, alone throughout the ancient world— the Jews held fast, through all temptation and disaster, to the conviction that God creates evil as well as good, or, in more pictorial language, that he planted the tree of the knowledge of good and evil. The two statements are one and the same, because for an omnipotent creator knowing and creating are indistinguishable, and also because evil itself cannot exist apart from the knowledge of it—that is why it is truly said that evil came into the world through man, because consciousness or self-knowledge came into the world with man. To eat of the tree of knowledge is to become man; for a being without knowledge of good and evil is not man. Yet evil existed before Adam, because God knew it; and because he knew it—indeed by knowing it— he (as Isaiah says) 'created' it. So finally, since nothing comes from nothing, evil and good must be of the nature of God himself. If the universe is God's universe, the evil in the universe is God's evil, and what we call 'the problem of evil' is God's problem.

I suppose no one ever seriously applied his mind to the drama of salvation—Adam's fall and his descendants' redemption by the Second Adam—without a sensation of repugnance. It seems as though the whole thing was a rather cruel and unnecessary theatre-play which the Almighty organized—perhaps for his entertainment during one of the tedious watches of eternity. All right, Adam was endowed with free will and he was disobedient. All right, it is very naughty to be disobedient and of course that started all the trouble. Yet God, being omnipotent and omniscient, knew perfectly well what Adam would do with his free will. So it was really God himself who must have deliberately triggered off the whole ghastly business.

As usual when we find ourselves in this sort of embarrassment, the way out is to face it directly instead of running away to hide. Isaiah does not deny it: 'I create evil' says his Yahweh. Genesis does not deny it: 'God caused the tree of knowledge of good and evil to grow' says the creation story. What hinders us, perhaps, in hearing what is being said is that word 'disobedience', ingeminated in our English minds by those first lines of *Paradise Lost*:

> Of man's first disobedience and the fruit
> Of that forbidden tree whose mortal taste
> Brought death into the world and all our woe . . .

Did you notice that word 'first', which Milton slipped in there, 'man's *first* disobedience'? It is terribly misleading. Since Adam had no knowledge of good or evil before tasting the fruit, his 'disobedience' in tasting it could not be sinful or wrong, because sin implies prior knowledge of good and evil. Sin was not the cause of the fall—that is illogical and self-contradictory—it was the result or concomitant of the fall. Or, to eliminate the misleading word 'fall' (with its overtones of descent and even of prostitution), sin was the result or concomitant of the acquisition of self-consciousness, whereby man was separated from the rest of creation to share with God in the knowledge of good and evil.

With the appearance of man, the evil as well as the good in the world became self-conscious; that became explicit which before was implicit or latent. Evil came into existence as a problem. How is it to be solved? How are good and evil to be reconciled? How is the conflict to be lived with? The universe, having acquired a human voice, cries out with Romans (1.24): 'O wretched man that I am! Who shall deliver me from the body of this death?' So we learn to see the drama of salvation and atonement no longer as a contrived puppet-play enacted on the narrow stage of Archbishop Ussher's 4004 years from creation to Christmas. The drama of man's salvation becomes the drama of the universe. If it were not too greatly daring, one could say that the drama of man's salvation is nothing less than the drama of God's own salvation. Once rendered conscious in man, the good and evil of the universe can be solved, reconciled, lived with, by no lesser means that God himself, through the further revelation of the creator to the self-consciousness of creation.

The great Christian philosopher, Saint Anselm, who we may be proud to recall was an archbishop of Canterbury, gave to his ripest work, which he wrote in self-imposed exile, the title *Cur deus homo?* or literally, 'Why God man?' Being in Latin and not English, the title can dispense with a verb. That is what seems to make it so significant and so haunting. What was the understood verb, and is it past or is it present? If it is past, 'Why God *became* man', when was the becoming? Was it at the fall or at the incarnation?

I think we have lost greatly by the disuse in the Anglican church, following no doubt upon the disuse in the Roman church, of the custom of reciting the beginning of St John's Gospel, silently or aloud, at the end of Mass. For at that recurrent moment, more perhaps than at any other in our lives, we need to be reminded that the Word, by which God created good and evil, is not only the Word which became flesh and dwelt among us but the light which lighteth every man that cometh into the world. God who creates evil is also God who was and is crucified and is also God who is within us. By nothing less than the truth of the Indivisible Trinity is the problem of evil solved. The writer of Romans answers his own question: 'I thank God through Jesus Christ our Lord. So then with the mind I myself serve the law of God but with the flesh the law of sin.'

INDEX OF BIBLICAL REFERENCES

INDEX

INDEX